The Delia Collection
Soup

BBC
BOOKS

Published by BBC Books
BBC Worldwide Ltd
Woodlands
80 Wood Lane
London W12 OTT

First published in 2003
Reprinted 2003

A proportion of these recipes has been
published previously in *Delia Smith's Winter
Collection*, *Delia Smith's Summer Collection*,
Delia's How To Cook Books One, *Two* and *Three*,
*Delia Smith's Complete Illustrated Cookery
Course*, *Delia Smith's Christmas*, *Delia's Red Nose
Collection* and *Delia's Vegetarian Collection*.

Edited for BBC Worldwide Ltd
by New Crane Ltd

Editor: Sarah Randell
Designer: Paul Webster
Sub-editor: Heather Cupit
Picture Editor: Diana Hughes
Recipe Testing: Pauline Curran
Commissioning Editor for the BBC: Vivien Bowler

ISBN 0 563 487305

Printed and bound in Italy
by L.E.G.O SpA
Colour separation by Radstock Reproductions Ltd
Midsomer Norton

Cover and title-page photographs: Michael Paul
For further photographic credits, see page 136

Introduction

When I look back over my years of cookery writing, I have to admit that very often, decisions about what to do have sprung from what my own particular needs are. As a very busy person, who has to work, run a home and cook, I felt it was extremely useful to have, for instance, summer recipes in one book – likewise winter and Christmas, giving easy access to those specific seasons.

This, my latest venture, has come about for similar reasons. Thirty three years of recipe writing have produced literally thousands of recipes. So I now feel what would be really helpful is to create a kind of ordered library (so I don't have to rack my brains and wonder which book this or that recipe is in!). Thus, if I want to make a soup, I don't have to look through the soup sections of various books, but have the whole lot in one convenient collection. Similarly, if I've managed to get hold of some veal shanks, I can go straight for the Italian collection, and so on.

In compiling these collections, I have chosen what I think are the best and most popular recipes and, at the same time, have added some that are completely new. It is my hope that those who have not previously tried my recipes will now have smaller collections to sample, and that those dedicated followers will appreciate an ordered library to provide easy access and a reminder of what has gone before and may have been forgotten.

Delia Smith

Conversion Tables

All these are approximate conversions, which have either been rounded up or down. In a few recipes it has been necessary to modify them very slightly. Never mix metric and imperial measures in one recipe, stick to one system or the other.

All spoon measurements used throughout this book are level unless specified otherwise.

All butter is salted unless specified otherwise.

All recipes have been double-tested, using a standard convection oven. If you are using a fan oven, adjust the cooking temperature according to the manufacturer's handbook.

Weights

½ oz	10 g
¾	20
1	25
1½	40
2	50
2½	60
3	75
4	110
4½	125
5	150
6	175
7	200
8	225
9	250
10	275
12	350
1 lb	450
1 lb 8 oz	700
2	900
3	1.35 kg

Volume

2 fl oz	55 ml
3	75
5 (¼ pint)	150
10 (½ pint)	275
1 pint	570
1¼	725
1¾	1 litre
2	1.2
2½	1.5
4	2.25

Dimensions

⅛ inch	3 mm
¼	5
½	1 cm
¾	2
1	2.5
1¼	3
1½	4
1¾	4.5
2	5
2½	6
3	7.5
3½	9
4	10
5	13
5¼	13.5
6	15
6½	16
7	18
7½	19
8	20
9	23
9½	24
10	25.5
11	28
12	30

Oven temperatures

Gas mark 1	275°F	140°C
2	300	150
3	325	170
4	350	180
5	375	190
6	400	200
7	425	220
8	450	230
9	475	240

Contents

Spring

Minestrone with Macaroni
Serves 6

2 oz (50 g) smoked streaky bacon or pancetta, derinded and finely chopped

1 medium onion, finely chopped

2 celery stalks, trimmed, washed and finely chopped

6 oz (175 g) carrots, washed and finely chopped

2 medium, ripe tomatoes, peeled and chopped

1 clove garlic, crushed

8 oz (225 g) leeks

6 oz (175 g) green cabbage, washed and finely shredded

3 oz (75 g) shortcut macaroni

1 oz (25 g) butter

1 tablespoon olive oil

2½ pints (1.5 litres) good chicken or vegetable stock

1 dessertspoon tomato purée

2 tablespoons chopped fresh parsley

1½ tablespoons chopped fresh basil

salt and freshly milled black pepper

To serve

lots of freshly grated Parmesan

If you have a food processor, it makes very light work of chopping the vegetables. But use the pulse button so you don't chop them too small. For a change, you can replace the macaroni with Italian risotto rice. Either way, serve it with lots of freshly grated Parmesan.

First of all, heat the butter and oil in a large saucepan, then add the bacon or pancetta and cook this for a minute or two before adding the onion, followed by the celery and carrots and then the tomatoes. Now stir in the crushed garlic and some salt and pepper, then cover and cook very gently for 20 minutes or so to allow the vegetables to sweat – give it an occasional stir to prevent the vegetables sticking.

Then pour in the stock and bring to the boil and then simmer gently, covered, for about 1 hour. To prepare the leeks, first take the tough green ends off and throw them out, then make a vertical split about halfway down the centre of each one and clean them by running them under the cold water tap while you fan out the layers – this will rid them of any hidden dust and grit. Then finely chop them.

When the hour is up, stir the leeks, cabbage, macaroni and tomato purée into the stock and cook, uncovered, for a further 10 minutes or until the pasta is cooked. Finally, stir in the parsley and basil and serve the minestrone in warmed soup bowls, sprinkled with Parmesan cheese.

Scallop Cream Soup
Serves 4-6

12 oz (350 g) scallops, with or without the roes

3 fl oz (75 ml) double cream

2 oz (50 g) butter

1 medium onion, finely chopped

1 lb (450 g) potatoes, peeled and diced

1 pint (570 ml) hot fish stock

10 fl oz (275 ml) cold milk

2 large egg yolks

salt and freshly milled black pepper

To serve

croutons (see page 129)

chopped fresh parsley

This really is one of the most luxurious and delicate soups imaginable. It is very easy to prepare and cook, but perfect for a special occasion.

First, melt the butter in a fairly large saucepan, add the onion and cook it very gently without colouring it at all, about 10 minutes. Next, add the diced potatoes, mix them in with the butter and onions and season with salt and pepper. Then, keeping the heat very low, put the lid on the pan and leave the mixture to sweat for another 10-15 minutes. After that pour in the hot fish stock, give it a good stir, cover the pan again and leave to simmer gently for a further 10-15 minutes.

Meanwhile, you can prepare the scallops: wash and dry them thoroughly and cut off the coral-coloured bits of roe (if using) – chop these and keep them on one side on a separate plate. The white parts should be diced roughly, put in a saucepan with the cold milk and a little salt and pepper, then poached very gently for 3-4 minutes or until opaque.

When the vegetables are cooked, transfer them and their cooking liquid to a blender and whiz to a purée. Now combine the white parts of the scallops (and the milk they were cooked in) with the potato purée. At this point any pieces of coral roe (if using) can be added and the soup gently re-heated.

Finally, beat the egg yolks thoroughly with the cream, remove the soup pan from the heat, stir in the egg and cream mixture and return the pan to a gentle heat. Cook, stirring, until the soup thickens slightly – but be very careful not to let it come anywhere near the boil or it will curdle. This final stage should only be done at the last minute, just before serving, so if you want to make this soup in advance, prepare it up to the egg yolk and cream stage.

To serve the soup, ladle it into warm soup bowls and garnish with croutons and some chopped fresh parsley.

Asparagus Soup
Serves 6

2 lb (900 g) asparagus

2 oz (50 g) butter

1 medium onion, finely chopped

1 slightly rounded tablespoon plain flour

1¾ pints (1 litre) hot chicken stock

5 fl oz (150 ml) double cream or crème fraîche

salt and freshly milled black pepper

This elegant soup is perfect to make when asparagus comes into season in spring. It can be served hot or very well chilled.

Prepare the asparagus by cutting away and discarding the tough, stringy white ends of the stalks, reserve 12 asparagus tips to garnish the soup, then chop the green parts of the rest of the asparagus into 1 inch (2.5 cm) lengths.

Next, melt the butter in a large saucepan over a gentle heat and cook the chopped onion in it for 5 minutes, keeping the heat low to prevent the onion colouring. Stir the asparagus into the melted butter and onion, then put a lid on and let it sweat for about 10 minutes, giving it a stir now and then.

Sprinkle in the tablespoon of flour, stir again to soak up the juices and add the hot chicken stock, a little at a time, stirring after each addition.

When all the stock is in, bring to simmering point, season with salt and freshly milled black pepper and keeping the heat low, let the soup barely simmer, partially covered, for 20 to 25 minutes.

Now you need to let the soup cool a little, then pour it into a blender and blend in batches (a large bowl is helpful here). Taste to check the seasoning. Finally, stir in the double cream or crème fraîche and the reserved asparagus tips. Re-heat gently for 3-4 minutes and serve very hot in warm soup bowls or alternatively, cool and chill thoroughly before serving in chilled bowls.

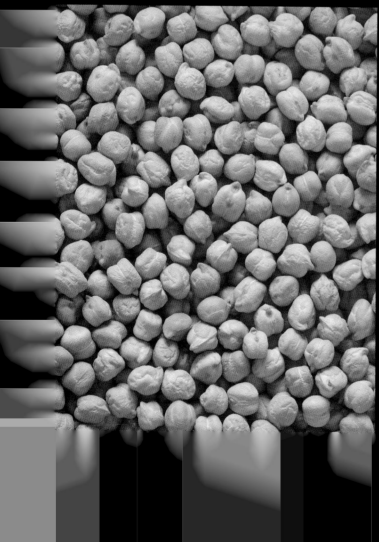

Chickpea, Chilli and Coriander Soup
Serves 4-6

8 oz (225 g) dried chickpeas, soaked overnight in twice their volume of cold water

2 small red chillies, halved, deseeded and chopped

½ oz (10 g) fresh coriander, leaves and stalks separated

1 tablespoon coriander seeds

1 tablespoon cumin seeds

2 oz (50 g) butter

6 fat cloves garlic, finely chopped

1 teaspoon ground turmeric

grated zest of 1 lemon, plus 2-3 tablespoons lemon juice

7 fl oz (200 ml) crème fraîche, to serve

salt and freshly milled black pepper

For the garnish

1 mild fat red or green chilli, deseeded and cut into very fine hair-like shreds

reserved coriander leaves (see above)

This has decidedly Mexican overtones. It isn't too hot and spicy but the presence of the chilli does give it a nice kick, and the flavour and texture of chickpeas is perfect for soup.

First of all, drain the chickpeas in a colander, rinse them under the cold tap, then place them in a large (6 pint/3.5 litre) saucepan with 2¾ pints (1.6 litres) of boiling, unsalted water. Then bring them up to simmering point, put a lid on and cook them very gently for about 1 hour or until the chickpeas are absolutely tender and squashy.

While they're cooking, prepare the rest of the soup ingredients. The coriander seeds and cumin seeds should be dry-roasted in a small pre-heated pan for 2-3 minutes, or until fragrant, then crushed in a pestle and mortar.

After that, melt the butter in the pan, add the crushed spices, along with the chopped garlic and chillies and cook over a low heat for about 5 minutes. Now add the turmeric, stir and heat that gently before removing the pan from the heat.

As soon as the chickpeas are tender, drain them in a colander placed over a bowl to reserve the cooking water. Transfer the chickpeas to a blender, together with a couple of ladles of cooking water, and purée them until fine and smooth. Now add the lemon zest, coriander stalks, and spices from the pan, along with another ladleful of cooking water, and blend once more until fine and smooth.

Next, the whole lot needs to go back into the saucepan with the rest of the reserved cooking water. Bring it all up to a gentle simmer, give it a good stir, season, then simmer gently for a further 30 minutes. All this can be done in advance, then, when you're ready to serve the soup, re-heat very gently without letting it come to the boil. Stir in half the crème fraîche and the lemon juice, taste to check the seasoning, then serve in hot soup bowls with the rest of the crème fraîche swirled in. Scatter with the shredded chilli and coriander leaves before serving.

Bloody Mary Soup
Serves 2

3 ripe tomatoes (6 oz/175 g)

18 fl oz (510 ml) fresh tomato juice

1 tablespoon Worcestershire sauce

1 tablespoon balsamic vinegar

juice of 1 lime

4 drops of Tabasco sauce

salt and freshly milled
black pepper

For the garnish

2 rounded dessertspoons
Greek yoghurt

a few sprigs of watercress

celery salt

Or, for the salsa

1 medium, ripe tomato

3 inch (7.5 cm) piece of celery

2 teaspoons vodka

¼ teaspoon celery salt

2 dashes of Tabasco sauce

More of a Virgin Mary really, but there's nothing to stop you adding a shot of vodka if you have the mind to. I sometimes serve this with a salsa, so have included the recipe – but it is not essential. And the very best news is not only is this soup low in fat but it must easily be the fastest soup on record.

First, put the kettle on, then place the 3 tomatoes (plus the one for the salsa if you are making it) in a heatproof bowl, pour boiling water over them and leave for 1 minute. After that, pour off the water and slip off the skins (protecting your hands with a cloth, if necessary). Now set aside the tomato for the salsa (if using). Either way, chop the rest of the tomatoes very finely, then add the whole lot to a medium saucepan. Bring the tomatoes up to a gentle simmer and let them cook for about 3 minutes. Next, pour in the tomato juice and the rest of the soup ingredients and season with salt and pepper. Do a bit of tasting here – it might need a dash more Tabasco or another squeeze of lime.

If you're making the salsa, cut the reserved, skinned tomato in half, then squeeze out the seeds and dice the flesh. Then mix the tomato and the celery with the remaining ingredients.

Now bring the soup back up to simmering point, then ladle it into warm soup bowls straightaway. To garnish, either quickly swirl a rounded dessertspoon of Greek yoghurt into each one, then add a sprig of watercress, a generous sprinkling of celery salt and serve. Or, if you've made the salsa, spoon half of it on to the top of each serving. On diet days I like to serve this soup with Ryvita biscuits spread with fromage frais or quark.

Smoked Haddock Chowder with Poached Quails' Eggs
Serves 4

1 lb 4 oz (570 g) undyed, smoked haddock, cut into 4 pieces

8 quails' eggs (or 4 hens' eggs)

18 fl oz (510 ml) milk

1 bay leaf

1½ oz (40 g) butter

1 medium onion, finely chopped

1 oz (25 g) plain flour

1 tablespoon lemon juice

1 tablespoon chopped fresh, flat-leaf parsley

salt and freshly milled black pepper

Smoked haddock makes a very fine soup, and this I've adapted from a famous version invented in Scotland, where it is called Cullen Skink. If you add poached quails' eggs to the soup, this makes a delightful surprise as you lift up an egg on your spoon. For a main-course meal you could use poached hens' eggs to make it more substantial. Either way, serve in warmed, shallow soup bowls with brown bread and butter.

Start by placing the haddock pieces in a large (6 pint/3.5 litre) saucepan, pour in the milk and 18 fl oz (510 ml) water, season with pepper (but no salt yet) and add the bay leaf. Now gently bring it up to simmering point and simmer very gently for 5 minutes before taking it off the heat and pouring it all into a bowl to steep for 15 minutes.

Meanwhile, wipe the saucepan with kitchen paper and melt the butter, add the chopped onion and let it sweat very gently, without browning, for about 10 minutes. By that time the haddock will be ready, so remove it with a draining spoon (reserving the liquid) to a board, discard the bay leaf, and peel off the skin. Next, stir the flour into the pan to soak up the juices, then gradually add the reserved fish-cooking liquid, stirring after each addition. When that's all in, add half the haddock, separated into flakes. Now allow the soup to cool a little, then pour it into a blender or food processor and blend thoroughly. After that, pass it through a sieve back into the saucepan, pressing through any solid bits of haddock that are left, to extract all the flavour. Discard what's left in the sieve, then separate the remaining haddock into flakes and add these to the soup. Taste it and season with salt, pepper and lemon juice and leave to one side to keep warm.

Now poach the eggs: pour boiling water straight into a medium frying pan and place over a heat gentle enough for there to be the merest trace of bubbles simmering on the base of the pan. Break the 8 quails' eggs (or 4 hens' eggs) into the water and let them cook for just 1 minute. Then remove the pan from the heat and let the quails' eggs stand in the water for 3 minutes, and the hens' eggs for 10, after which time the whites will be set and the yolks creamy. Use a draining spoon and a wad of kitchen paper underneath to remove the eggs, place 2 quails' eggs (or 1 hens' egg) in each warmed serving bowl, ladle the soup on top and serve, sprinkled with the chopped parsley.

Shiitake Broth with Sesame Toast
Serves 6

8 oz (225 g) shiitake mushrooms

3 oz (75 g) open-cap mushrooms

½ oz (10 g) dried shiitake mushrooms

1 tablespoon groundnut or other flavourless oil

2 medium onions, finely chopped

3 pints (1.75 litres) miso stock made with 2 x 18 g sachets instant miso soup paste mixed with boiling water

2 tablespoons white basmati rice

2 dessertspoons arrowroot

4 spring onions, finely chopped

salt and freshly milled black pepper

For the sesame toast

6 medium-cut slices from a large white loaf, crusts removed

softened butter, for spreading

1½ oz (40 g) sesame seeds

This is a lovely light soup without too many calories made with Japanese miso stock and dried shiitake mushrooms, which have a strong flavour, but just the fresh shiitake mushrooms can be used, if you prefer.

First of all, rinse the dried shiitake mushrooms in a sieve under cold running water, then place them in a heatproof bowl and put 1 pint (570 ml) of the hot miso stock over them. Then just leave them to soak and soften for about 30 minutes. Meanwhile, finely chop the fresh shiitake and open-cap mushrooms. When the dried mushrooms have had their soaking time, line a sieve with a double layer of kitchen paper, place it over a bowl and strain the mushrooms, reserving the liquid. Squeeze them to remove any excess liquid, then chop them fairly finely. Now heat the oil in a large saucepan, then add the chopped onions and fry gently for about 10 minutes or until softened. Next, add the fresh and the strained dried mushrooms, stir them around in the oil and cook for a minute or two. Then pour in the mushroom soaking liquid and the rest of the miso stock and bring to simmering point. Sprinkle in the rice, stirring occasionally, to prevent the rice from sticking. Simmer gently, uncovered, for 25 minutes or until the rice is just tender.

Meanwhile, you can start to make the sesame toast. Pre-heat the grill to its highest setting. Then toast the slices of bread on one side only. Now butter them on the untoasted side, right up to the edges, and sprinkle a tablespoonful of sesame seeds over each slice to cover as evenly as possible, pressing the seeds down so they will stay in position. Towards the end of the soup's cooking time, in a small basin, blend the arrowroot (which will thicken the soup) with 2 dessertspoons of cold water until smooth. Then, when the soup is ready, add the blended arrowroot, together with three-quarters of the finely chopped spring onions and, stirring continuously, bring back to simmering point and simmer for 1 minute. Season to taste. To finish making the toast, return the bread to the grill. Toast the sesame-encrusted side until the seeds are lightly toasted and the bread itself goes golden brown. Then cut each slice up into four squares and eat straight-away with the piping hot soup, garnished with the remaining spring onions.

Carrot and Coriander Soup
Serves 6

2 lb (900 g) carrots,
peeled and chopped

1 tablespoon coriander seeds

1 oz (25 g) butter

1 small clove garlic, crushed

2 pints (1.2 litres) chicken
or vegetable stock

3 tablespoons chopped fresh
coriander, plus 6 small sprigs,
to garnish

3 tablespoons crème fraîche

salt and freshly milled
black pepper

This is a lovely soup to make with spring carrots that are not quite as sweet as those in the summer. Coriander is said to have the flavour of roasted orange peel, which makes the two perfect partners. Serve the soup with plenty of warm crusty bread.

Begin by dry-roasting the coriander seeds in a small frying pan over a medium heat, stirring and tossing them around for 1-2 minutes, or until they begin to look toasted and start to jump in the pan. Now tip them into a pestle and mortar and crush them coarsely.

Next, heat the butter in a large saucepan, then add the chopped carrots, garlic and three-quarters of the crushed coriander seeds. Stir the carrots in the buttery juices and crushed seeds, then cover the pan and let the vegetables cook over a gentle heat until they are beginning to soften – about 10 minutes.

Next, add the stock and season with salt and pepper and bring everything up to the boil. Then reduce the heat to low and simmer for a further 15-20 minutes, partially covered, or until all the vegetables are tender. Leave the soup to cool a little, then you can liquidise the whole lot in batches (a large bowl to put each batch in is helpful here). After that, return the purée to the pan and stir in the chopped fresh coriander and 2 tablespoons of the crème fraîche. Re-heat the soup, then taste to check the seasoning and serve in warmed bowls and garnish each one with a swirl of crème fraîche, a sprinkling of the remaining toasted coriander seeds and a sprig of fresh coriander.

Roasted Tomato Soup with Purée of Basil and Olive Croutons
Serves 4

1 lb 8 oz (700 g) medium, ripe, red tomatoes, skinned

1 small bunch fresh basil leaves (¾ oz/20 g)

3-4 tablespoons extra virgin olive oil

1 fat clove garlic, chopped

4 oz (110 g) potato

1 heaped teaspoon tomato purée

1 teaspoon balsamic vinegar

salt and freshly milled black pepper

For the olive croutons

4 medium slices of Italian ciabatta bread, cubed

1 tablespoon olive oil

1 dessertspoon olive paste

You will also need a solid, shallow roasting tray, about 13 x 13 inches (33 x 33 cm).

Pre-heat the oven to gas mark 5, 375°F (190°C).

At first you're going to think, 'Why bother to roast tomatoes just for soup?', but I promise you that once you've tasted the difference you'll know it's worth it – especially in the spring when it's hard to get really ripe, full-flavoured tomatoes. And roasting really isn't any trouble, it just means time in the oven.

Slice each tomato in half, arrange the halves on the roasting tray, cut side uppermost, and season with salt and pepper. Sprinkle a few droplets of olive oil on to each one, followed by the chopped garlic, and finally, top each one with a piece of basil leaf (dipping the basil in oil first to get a good coating). Now pop the whole lot into the oven and roast the tomatoes for 50 minutes-1 hour or until the edges are slightly blackened – what happens in this process is that the liquid in the tomatoes evaporates and concentrates their flavour, as do the toasted edges. (Instead of chopped garlic, you can roast a few whole small cloves.) About 20 minutes before the end of the roasting time, peel and chop the potato, place it in a saucepan with some salt, 15 fl oz (425 ml) boiling water and the tomato purée and simmer for 20 minutes. For the croutons, place the bread cubes in a bowl, with the olive oil and olive paste, and stir them around to get a good coating of both. Then arrange the croutons on a small baking sheet and bake in the oven for 8-10 minutes (put a timer on). Leave to cool on the baking sheet.

When the tomatoes are ready, scrape them with all their juices and crusty bits into a food processor (a spatula is best for this), then when the contents of the potato saucepan have cooled a little, add these too and whiz everything to a not-too-uniform purée. You can now sieve out the seeds but I prefer to leave them in, as I like the texture. (If you're using whole garlic cloves, squeeze the roasted garlic from the skin into the processor when you whiz the tomatoes.) Just before serving the soup – which should be re-heated very gently, make the basil purée by stripping the remaining leaves into a mortar, sprinkling with ¼ teaspoon of salt, then bashing the leaves down with the pestle. It takes a minute or two for the leaves to collapse down and become a purée, at which point add 2 tablespoons of olive oil and the balsamic vinegar and stir well. Serve each bowl of soup, garnished with a swirl of purée and a few croutons.

Spinach Soup with Fontina
Serves 4

14 oz (400 g) prepared leaf spinach

3 oz (75 g) Fontina or Gruyère cheese, cut into ¼ inch (5 mm) dice

2 oz (50 g) butter

2 shallots, chopped

14 oz (400 g) potatoes, peeled and cut into ½ inch (1 cm) cubes

1¼ pints (725 ml) vegetable stock

a generous grating of fresh nutmeg

7 fl oz (200 ml) crème fraîche

chopped fresh parsley
or finely chopped fresh chives,
to garnish

salt and freshly milled
black pepper

We think Italian Fontina cheese, which has a melting creaminess, is the best to use in this soup but if you can't get hold of it, then Gruyère is almost as good.

Begin by melting the butter in a large saucepan and then add the shallots and potatoes. Stir everything together in the buttery juices, then cover the saucepan and cook the shallots and potato very gently for 10 minutes. Next, add the stock and bring to simmering point. Let everything simmer for another 5-10 minutes or until the potato is tender. Now add the spinach leaves, cover with a lid and allow them to collapse in the heat of the pan. Then stir everything together and add a generous grating of fresh nutmeg and season with salt and pepper. Once all the spinach has wilted, take the pan off the heat, leave it aside to cool a little, then blend the soup in batches until smooth (have a bowl ready to put the first batch in).

Then return the soup to the pan and stir in the crème fraîche. When you're ready to serve the soup, re-heat it gently just up to simmering point and finally, stir in the diced cheese. Ladle the hot soup into warm bowls and, if you like, garnish each one with a scattering of chopped parsley or finely chopped fresh chives.

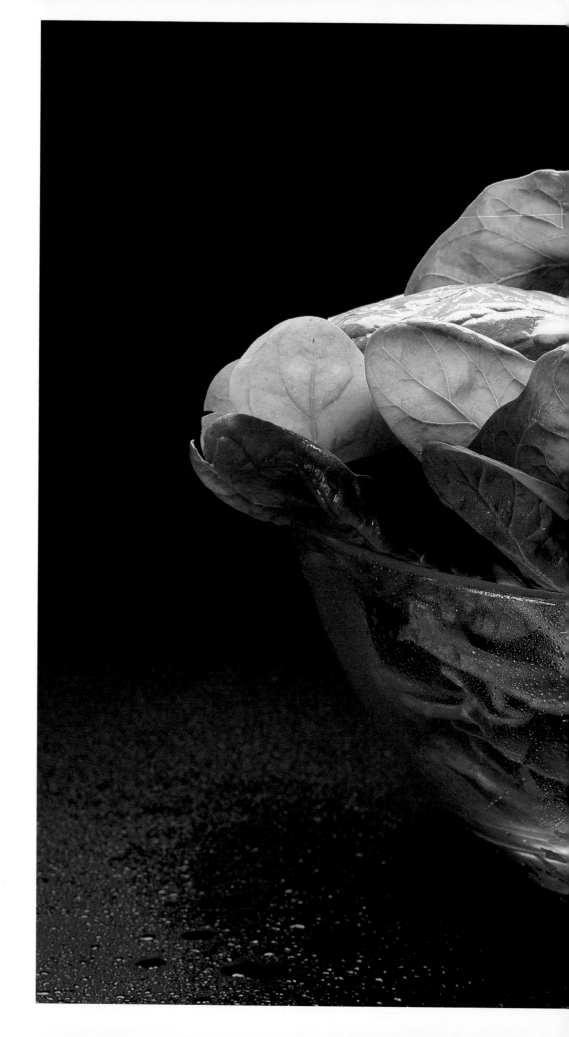

Hot and Sour Thai Chicken Broth
Serves 4

2 skinless chicken breasts
(6 oz/175 g each)

2 pints (1.2 litres) chicken stock

a small bunch of fresh coriander
(½ oz/10 g)

2 small red bird's-eye chillies

1 stalk of lemon grass,
roughly chopped

a small piece (1 inch/2.5 cm) of
ginger, peeled and sliced

2 medium, ripe tomatoes

3 spring onions, trimmed and finely
sliced (including the green parts)

2 oz (50 g) fresh, shelled peas

2 oz (50 g) sugar snap peas,
cut in half

1 tablespoon Thai fish sauce

1 tablespoon tamarind purée

juice of a large lime
(about 2 tablespoons)

This recipe, given to me by Sarah Randell, the Editor of the Collection, is based on a version of Tom Yum soup - a spicy, clear, refreshing broth found on the menu of most Thai restaurants. This one is made with chicken but it is also delicious made with tiger prawns – and what's more, it is low in fat. The Thai fish sauce is used to season the soup but make sure you buy a good-quality version, such as Squid, as some less authentic brands are excessively salty. This soup is also nice made with Japanese miso stock.

First of all, you need to pick all the coriander leaves off the stalks and then cut 1 of the chillies in half lengthways and deseed it. Next, put the chicken stock into a large saucepan and add the coriander stalks, halved chilli, lemon grass and ginger. Bring the mixture to the boil, give everything a stir, then cover and leave to simmer very gently for 15 minutes to allow the Thai flavours to infuse the stock. You can make this stock in advance but add the rest of the ingredients shortly before serving.

Meanwhile, place the tomatoes in a bowl and pour boiling water over them and leave them for 1 minute before draining. Next, skin the tomatoes and cut each one into quarters, then remove the seeds and cut each quarter into three lengthways, so you end up with thin slices. Now cut each chicken breast in half widthways and then slice each half into five or six long thin strips and then slice each of these in half lengthways so you end up with thin slivers of chicken. Now strain the stock into a colander set over a bowl and discard the flavourings. Next, return the stock to the pan and when it is back to simmering point, stir in the thin slivers of chicken, and half of the spring onions. Stir and then cover again and leave the chicken to poach gently for 5 minutes or until it is cooked through. Meanwhile, trim and halve the remaining chilli, remove the seeds, and then finely slice it, making sure you wash your hands afterwards.

Next, add the peas, sugar snaps, sliced chilli, fish sauce, tamarind and lime juice to the soup, stir and gently simmer for 2-3 minutes or until the peas are just tender but still retain their bite. Stir the slices of tomato in at the last minute and then divide the coriander leaves among four deep bowls. Ladle the piping hot soup on top, sprinkle with the remaining spring onions and serve immediately.

Summer

Ajo Blanco (chilled almond soup)
Serves 4

7 oz (200 g) unblanched almonds, preferably Spanish almonds (never ready-blanched for this recipe)

7-8 fl oz (200-225 ml) olive oil, preferably Spanish

3 cloves garlic

1 dessertspoon sherry vinegar

2 teaspoons salt, or more, to taste

To serve

8 ice cubes

4 oz (110 g) black or green grapes, deseeded and halved

1 dessert apple, peeled, cored and thinly sliced

This supremely wonderful recipe for Chilled Almond Soup, generously laced with garlic, was given to me by my friend Neville who has a house in Andalucia surrounded by almond trees. It can be made up to five days ahead – and, as Neville says, it goes on improving in flavour.

First, you need to blanch the almonds. To do this, place them in a heatproof bowl, pour in enough boiling water to cover, then leave them aside for 3-4 minutes. Now drain them in a colander and simply squeeze the nuts out of their skins into the bowl.

After that, put the almonds in a blender and pour in the olive oil. (The oil should just cover the almonds – if it doesn't, add a little more.) Then peel and add the garlic, the vinegar and salt and liquidise until everything is smooth. Now, with the motor still running, slowly add about 12 fl oz (340 ml) of cold water. Pour the soup into a large bowl and if it seems too thick, add a little more water. Then cover the bowl with cling-film and keep it well chilled until you're ready to serve.

Just before serving, stir in the ice cubes and ladle the soup into chilled bowls. Garnish with the grapes and apple slices.

Old English Summer Soup
Serves 4

12 oz (350 g) potatoes, peeled and finely diced

4 or 5 spring onions, finely chopped (including the green parts)

1 small round lettuce, washed, patted dry and shredded

½ medium cucumber, chopped (no need to peel)

3 oz (75 g) butter

1½ pints (850 ml) chicken or vegetable stock

snipped fresh chives, to garnish

salt and freshly milled black pepper

This is a helpful recipe for gardeners whose summer crop of vegetables threatens to overwhelm them. If you like, you can serve this soup cold in chilled bowls in really hot weather. Either way, it is a lovely soup to serve on a summer's day.

First of all, in a medium saucepan, melt the butter gently, then add the potatoes, spring onions, lettuce and cucumber. Stir everything round in the butter, then, keeping the heat very low, put a lid on and let everything sweat for 10 minutes.

Now pour in the stock, stir, add some salt and freshly milled black pepper and bring to the boil. Then reduce the heat to low, put the lid on and let it simmer gently for another 20 minutes. Leave the soup to cool a little, then purée the whole lot in a blender. If you need to do this in two batches, it is helpful to have a bowl to hand to put the first batch in. Finally, check the seasoning, gently re-heat the soup and serve it with the freshly snipped chives stirred in at the last moment or sprinkle a few into each bowl.

Chilled Spanish Gazpacho
Serves 6

1 lb 8 oz (700 g) firm, ripe, red tomatoes

4 inch (10 cm) piece of cucumber, peeled and chopped

2 or 3 spring onions, chopped

2 cloves garlic, crushed

½ large red or green pepper, deseeded and chopped

1 heaped teaspoon chopped fresh basil, marjoram or thyme (depending on what's available)

4 tablespoons olive oil

1½ tablespoons wine vinegar

salt and freshly milled black pepper

For the garnish

½ large red or green pepper, deseeded and very finely chopped

4 inch (10 cm) piece of cucumber, peeled and finely chopped

2 spring onions, finely chopped

1 egg, hard-boiled and finely chopped

1 heaped tablespoon chopped fresh parsley

salt and freshly milled black pepper

To serve

4 ice cubes

small croutons (see page 129)

This is a truly beautiful soup for serving ice cold during the summer and it's particularly refreshing if we're lucky enough to have hot weather. However, please don't attempt to make it in the winter as the flavourless, unseasonal salad vegetables and imported tomatoes will not do it justice.

Begin by placing the tomatoes in a bowl and pouring boiling water over them, leave for a minute and then the skins will loosen and slip off very easily (protect your hands with a cloth, if necessary). Halve the tomatoes, scoop out and discard the seeds and roughly chop the flesh.

Now place the tomatoes, cucumber, spring onions, crushed garlic and chopped pepper in a blender, adding a seasoning of salt and pepper, the herbs, oil and wine vinegar. Then blend everything at top speed until the soup is absolutely smooth. If your blender is very small, combine all the ingredients first, then blend in two or three batches; have a large bowl to hand to put the batches in as they are ready. Taste to check the seasoning and stir in a little cold water to thin it slightly – anything from 5-10 fl oz (150-275 ml) – then cover the bowl and chill.

To make the garnish, simply combine all the ingredients, together with a seasoning of salt and freshly milled black pepper, and hand them round at the table, together with small croutons of bread fried till crisp in olive oil, well drained and cooled. Serve the soup chilled with 4 ice cubes floating in it or set on a bed of ice.

Potato Soup with Wilted Leaves
Serves 6

1 lb 8 oz (700 g) new potatoes, peeled and diced

4 oz (110 g) mixed watercress, baby leaf spinach and rocket

3 oz (75 g) butter

1 lb (450 g) onions, chopped

1½ pints (850 ml) chicken or vegetable stock

10 fl oz (275 ml) milk

salt and freshly milled black pepper

This recipe was invented around one of those ready-mixed bags of watercress, baby spinach and rocket leaves. Otherwise, just make up the same quantity from your own selection.

In a large, thick-based saucepan, gently melt 2 oz (50 g) of the butter, then add the potatoes and onions, stirring them all around with a wooden spoon so they get a nice coating of butter. Season with salt and pepper, then cover and let the vegetables sweat over a very low heat for about 15 minutes, stirring everything now and then.

After that, add the stock and milk, bring to simmering point, cover and let the soup simmer very gently for a further 20 minutes or until the potatoes are soft – careful as, if you have the heat too high, the milk may cause it to boil over. Now allow the soup to cool a little, before putting the whole lot into a blender in batches and blend to a purée (a bowl to put each batch in is helpful here). Return the soup to the pan, then gently re-heat it, tasting to check the seasoning.

Meanwhile, roughly chop the watercress, spinach and rocket (including the stalks), and stir them into the soup with the remaining 1 oz (25 g) butter. As soon as the leaves have wilted, serve the soup in warm bowls.

Chilled Lemon Grass
and Coriander Vichyssoise
Serves 4

4 thick stems of lemon grass

2 oz (50 g) fresh coriander leaves

4 spring onions

2 oz (50 g) butter

2 medium onions, chopped

10 oz (275 g) new potatoes,
scraped and chopped small

5 fl oz (150 ml) milk

thin lemon slices, to garnish

salt and freshly milled
black pepper

Leeks, which have made vichyssoise famous, are not at their best in summer, but this alternative version is, I think, even better. In hot summer weather it's lovely made using fresh lemon grass, available in oriental shops and larger supermarkets. Remember to serve the soup icy cold in chilled soup bowls.

First of all, strip the coriander leaves from the stalks and reserve both the leaves and the stalks. Lemon grass is dealt with in exactly the same way as leeks: that is, you trim the root and the tough top away, leaving about 6 inches (15 cm) of stem, remove the outer skin and chop the lemon grass quite finely. Then do the same with the spring onions. Next, gather up all the trimmings from both, wash them and pop them into a saucepan, together with the coriander stalks, some salt and 1½ pints (850 ml) water and simmer, covered, for about 30 minutes to make a stock.

To make the soup, begin by melting the butter in a large saucepan, then add the chopped lemon grass, onions (reserve the spring onions till later) and potatoes and keeping the heat low, let the vegetables sweat gently, covered, for about 10 minutes. After that, pour in the stock through a strainer, discard the debris, then add the milk and about three-quarters of the coriander leaves. Season with salt and pepper, bring the soup up to simmering point and simmer very gently on a low heat, partially covered, for about 25 minutes.

Allow the soup to cool a little before pouring it into a food processor or blender, whiz it up, then pour it through a strainer into a bowl. If you need to blend the soup in batches, it's handy to have a bowl nearby to put the first batch in. When it is cold, cover and chill the soup thoroughly till you're ready to serve.

I think it's a good idea to serve the soup in glass bowls that have already been chilled. Add a cube of ice to each bowl and sprinkle in the rest of the coriander leaves (finely chopped) and the spring onions as a garnish. Finally, float some lemon slices on top and serve straightaway.

Fresh Tomato Soup with Basil, and Parmesan Croutons
Serves 4

1 lb 8 oz (700 g) ripe, red tomatoes, cut in quarters (leave the skin on)

1½ tablespoons olive oil

1 medium onion, chopped small

1 medium potato, peeled and chopped small

10 fl oz (275 ml) vegetable stock

1 clove garlic, crushed

salt and freshly milled black pepper

For the Parmesan croutons

2 oz (50 g) bread, cut into small cubes

1 tablespoon olive oil

1 dessertspoon freshly grated Parmesan

To serve

2 teaspoons chopped fresh basil, plus 4 small sprigs

2 rounded teaspoons crème fraîche

Pre-heat the oven to gas mark 4, 350°F (180°C).

When I first wrote on cookery, a reader wrote to the Editor of my newspaper, complaining my recipe for tomato soup didn't work. Rather conscientiously, the Editor took the recipe home to try. He then wrote to me saying, 'I've made your tomato soup and – it's absolutely delicious!' Serve this soup garnished with a swirl of crème fraîche, the croutons and a sprig of fresh basil.

Gently heat the olive oil in a heavy-bottomed saucepan, then put in the onion and potato and let them soften slowly without browning. This takes 10-15 minutes.

Now add the tomatoes, stir well, and let them cook for a minute. Pour the stock over the tomatoes, stir, season with salt and pepper and add the garlic. Cover and allow everything to simmer for 25 minutes.

Meanwhile, you can make the croutons. Just place the oil and cubes of bread in a small bowl, stir them around until the oil is soaked up, then sprinkle in the Parmesan. Stir the cubes around to coat them in that as well, then spread them on a baking sheet and bake on a high shelf in the oven for 10 minutes or until they are crisp and golden (do put a kitchen timer on because it's so easy to forget all about them). Then allow them to cool and leave them on one side until the soup has had its cooking time.

When the soup is ready, liquidise the whole lot in a blender or food processor and then pass the soup through a sieve to extract the skins and pips (if you need to blend the soup in batches, have a bowl to hand to put the first batch in). Now return the soup to the saucepan to re-heat, taste to check the seasoning and add the chopped basil. Serve with a swirl of crème fraîche, the croutons and a sprig of fresh basil. Alternatively, serve chilled.

Chilled Yoghurt and Cucumber Soup with Mint
Serves 4

10 fl oz (275 ml) natural yoghurt

2 medium, firm, young cucumbers

2 teaspoons chopped fresh mint

5 fl oz (150 ml) soured cream

1 clove garlic, crushed

2 teaspoons fresh lemon juice

a little milk, if needed

4 slices of lemon,
cut very thinly, to serve

salt and freshly milled
black pepper

This cool, light and subtle soup is incredibly easy and quick to make. However, it does need some fresh summer cucumbers in season for the best flavour of all.

First, peel the cucumbers thinly with a potato peeler, leaving some of the green skin on, then slice them. Reserve a few thin slices to garnish the soup, then place the rest in a blender, along with the yoghurt, soured cream and crushed garlic. Switch on and blend at the highest speed until smooth. Add a seasoning of salt and pepper and the lemon juice, then pour the soup into a tureen and if it seems to be a little too thick, thin it with some cold milk. Now stir in the chopped fresh mint, cover and chill very thoroughly for several hours before serving.

To serve, ladle the soup into individual chilled soup bowls and float a few thin slices of cucumber and a thin slice of lemon on each one.

Chilled Fennel Gazpacho with Olive Ciabatta Croutons
Serves 4

1 largish fennel bulb (12 oz/350 g)

1 lb 8 oz (700 g) ripe red tomatoes

¾ teaspoon coriander seeds

½ teaspoon mixed peppercorns

1 tablespoon extra virgin olive oil

1 small onion, chopped

1 large clove garlic, crushed

½ tablespoon balsamic vinegar

1 tablespoon lemon juice

¾ teaspoon chopped fresh oregano

1 teaspoon tomato purée

1 rounded teaspoon sea salt

To garnish

4 medium slices ciabatta bread (about 2 oz/50 g) each

1 tablespoon olive oil

1 dessertspoon olive paste

I've always loved gazpacho and never fail to order it when I'm in Spain or Portugal: it really is one of the nicest first courses when the weather is warm. This version is the same but different – the same refreshing, salady texture but with quite a different flavour. Serve warm if the weather's chilly, but if you are serving it cold, do make sure that it's really cold. Chill the bowls first and add some ice cubes just before serving.

First, skin the tomatoes: pour boiling water over them and leave for 1 minute before draining them and slipping off the skins (protect your hands with a cloth if they're too hot). Then chop the tomatoes roughly. Next, trim the green fronds from the fennel (reserve these for the garnish) and cut the bulb into quarters. Trim away a little of the central stem at the base and slice the fennel into thinnish slices. Now place these in a saucepan with the salt and measure in 15 fl oz (425 ml) of water. Bring it up to simmering point, then put a lid on and simmer gently for 10 minutes.

Meanwhile, crush the coriander seeds and mixed peppercorns in a pestle and mortar. Then heat the oil in a large saucepan and add the crushed spices, along with the chopped onion. Let these cook gently for 5 minutes, then add the crushed garlic and cook for a further 2 minutes. Now add the balsamic vinegar, lemon juice, chopped tomatoes and oregano, stir well, then add the fennel, along with the water in which it was simmering. Finally, stir in the tomato purée, bring everything up to simmering point and simmer gently, without a lid, for 30 minutes.

Meanwhile, pre-heat the oven to gas mark 5, 375°F (190°C). First, cut the bread into small cubes, then place them in a bowl, together with the olive oil and paste, and stir them around to get a good coating of both. Now arrange the croutons on a small baking sheet and put them in the oven to bake for 8-10 minutes – but please put on a timer for this as 10 minutes pass very quickly and croutons have a nasty habit of turning into cinders! Then leave to cool on the baking sheet. Cool the soup a little, then whiz to a purée in a blender (a bowl to put the first batch in is helpful here). When the soup has cooled completely, cover and chill for several hours. Serve, garnished with the olive croutons and the chopped green fennel fronds.

Watercress and Buttermilk Vichyssoise
Serves 8

12 oz (350 g) watercress (reserve a few leaves for garnishing)

10 fl oz (275 ml) buttermilk

4 oz (110 g) butter

the white parts of 3 leeks (about 12 oz/350 g), washed and chopped

1 medium onion, chopped small

1 lb 8 oz (700 g) new potatoes, peeled and chopped

3 pints (1.75 litres) vegetable stock

salt and freshly milled black pepper

This is a very summery, cool soup. The peppery, green watercress leaves are matched perfectly by the soothing acidity of buttermilk. It must be served very cold.

First of all, melt the butter in a large (6 pint/3.5 litre) saucepan, then add the prepared leeks, onion, potatoes and half of the watercress. Stir them around so that they're coated with the melted butter. Next, sprinkle in some salt, then cover with a lid and let the vegetables sweat over a very gentle heat for about 20 minutes, giving the mixture a good stir about halfway through.

After that, add the stock, bring everything up to simmering point and simmer, covered, for about 10-15 minutes or until the vegetables are quite tender. Then remove the pan from the heat and leave the soup to cool a little, then liquidise until it is smooth – you'll need to do this in batches. A bowl to put the first batch in is useful. Next, transfer the soup to a large bowl and leave until cold.

When the soup is cold, stir in three-quarters of the buttermilk and season to taste. Cover the bowl with clingfilm and chill the soup thoroughly before serving – overnight is ideal.

When you are ready to serve the soup, put the other half of the watercress in a large bowl. Then, using the end of a rolling pin or a pestle, 'bruise' the leaves – this will release the oil in the leaves. Now whiz the watercress in the blender with about a third of the chilled soup (remembering to reserve a few leaves for garnishing) and when it is smooth, stir it into the rest of the soup.

Serve the soup in bowls that have been very well chilled and garnish each one with a swirl of the remaining buttermilk and a few reserved watercress leaves.

Fresh Shelled Pea Soup
Serves 4

2 lb (900 g) fresh peas, shelled (weight after shelling is approximately 11 oz/315 g)

2 oz (50 g) butter

4 spring onions, finely chopped (including the green parts)

4 lettuce leaves, finely chopped

1 rasher unsmoked bacon, derinded and finely chopped

2 oz (50 g) fresh young leaf spinach

1 teaspoon caster sugar

1 tablespoon finely chopped fresh mint

1-2 tablespoons crème fraîche

freshly grated nutmeg

salt and freshly milled black pepper

This soup is a lovely dark green colour and has all the wonderful ingredients and flavours of peas *à la Française* – peas, spring onions, lettuce and bacon – blended into a velvety smooth soup.

First of all, in a large saucepan melt the butter and gently sauté the chopped spring onions, lettuce, bacon and spinach for about 5 minutes, then add the peas and some salt and stir everything together. Then pour in 1¼ pints (725 ml) boiling water from the kettle. Next, add the sugar, put on a lid and let the peas simmer gently for 10 to 15 minutes, or until they are soft.

Now allow the soup to cool a little, then whiz it to a purée in batches in a blender until smooth. You'll find it helpful to have a bowl handy to put the first batch in. Taste and season with more salt (if it needs it) and freshly milled black pepper, then gently re-heat. Stir the mint into the soup and serve in hot bowls, garnishing each one with a teaspoon of crème fraîche and a little freshly grated nutmeg just before serving.

Courgette Soup
with Watercress and Pecorino Pesto
Serves 4-6

1 lb (450 g) courgettes, diced with their skins left on

2 oz (50 g) butter

4 oz (110 g) potatoes, peeled and diced

1 large onion, chopped

1 clove of garlic, finely chopped

1½ pints (850 ml) chicken or vegetable stock

5 fl oz (150 ml) single cream

salt and freshly milled black pepper

For the pesto

2 oz (50 g) watercress

1 small clove garlic, crushed

1 tablespoon pine nuts

6 tablespoons extra virgin olive oil

1 oz (25 g) Pecorino Romano or Parmesan, grated

salt

This light summer soup is perfect for late summer when courgettes are cheap and plentiful. Serve each bowl with a spoonful of the watercress and pecorino pesto zigzagged over the surface of the soup.

Begin by melting the butter gently in a large saucepan, add the potatoes, courgettes, onion and garlic and stir everything around so the vegetables are glossy and covered in butter. Add a little salt and freshly milled black pepper, then partially cover the pan and leave the vegetables to sweat, to release the buttery juices, on a low heat for 15 minutes. Now add the stock, bring the soup back to simmering point and cook very gently for a further 7-10 minutes, again partially covered, or until the potatoes are soft and the courgettes are just tender.

While the soup is simmering, make the pesto. All you do is put the watercress (stalks and all), garlic, pine nuts and olive oil, together with some salt, in a food processor or blender and whiz until you have a smooth purée. Then transfer the purée to a bowl and stir in the grated Pecorino (or Parmesan) cheese.

When the soup is ready, cool it a little, then purée it in a blender until smooth – you will probably need to do this in two batches, so have a large bowl nearby to pour the first batch into. Next, put the whole lot back in the saucepan, stir in the cream, then gently re-heat the soup. Ladle it into bowls, top each one with a spoonful of the pesto and, using a skewer or the tip of a small knife, zigzag the pesto all over the surface of the soup.

Autumn

Leek, Onion and Potato Soup
Serves 4-6

4 large leeks

1 medium onion, chopped small

2 medium potatoes, peeled and diced

2 oz (50 g) butter

1½ pints (850 ml) vegetable stock

10 fl oz (275 ml) milk

salt and freshly milled black pepper

To serve

1½ tablespoons snipped fresh chives or chopped fresh parsley

2 tablespoons cream or crème fraîche

This has to be one of my own top of the pops favourites and has proven to be one of my most popular recipes with everyone over the years. The chilled version of this soup is a classic vichyssoise. Either way, it's an absolute winner.

Begin by trimming the leeks, discarding the tough outer layer. Now split them in half lengthways and slice them quite finely, then wash them thoroughly in two or three changes of water. Drain well. In a large, thick-based saucepan, gently melt the butter, then add the leeks, onion and potatoes, stirring them all around with a wooden spoon so they get a nice coating of butter. Season with salt and pepper, then cover and let the vegetables sweat over a very low heat for about 15 minutes.

After that, add the stock and milk, bring to simmering point, cover and let the soup simmer very gently for a further 20 minutes or until the vegetables are soft – if you have the heat too high the milk in it may cause it to boil over. Now you can put the whole lot into a blender – leave it to cool a little first - and blend to a purée. If you have to blend the soup in batches, make sure you have a bowl to hand to put the first batch into.

Now return the soup to the saucepan and re-heat gently, tasting to check the seasoning. Add a swirl of cream or crème fraîche before serving and sprinkle with freshly snipped chives or parsley.

Butternut Squash Soup with Toasted Sweetcorn
Serves 6

1 lb 8 oz (700 g) butternut squash, or pumpkin, peeled, deseeded and chopped into 1 inch (2.5 cm) dice

1 lb 4 oz (570 g) sweetcorn (off-the-cob weight, from 5-6 cobs)

1 oz (25 g) butter, plus 1 teaspoon melted butter, for the sweetcorn

1 medium onion, finely chopped

10 fl oz (275 ml) whole milk

1¼ pints (725 ml) vegetable stock

salt and freshly milled black pepper

This is a very fine combination: the soft, velvety texture of the butternut makes the soup deliciously creamy and the toasted sweetcorn provides contrasting flavour and crunch.

Begin by melting the butter in a medium (3 pint/1.75 litre) saucepan, then add the onion and soften it for about 8 minutes. After that, add the chopped butternut squash (or pumpkin), along with half the sweetcorn, then give everything a good stir and season with salt and pepper. Put the lid on and, keeping the heat low, allow the vegetables to sweat gently and release their juices – this should take about 10 minutes. Next, pour in the milk and stock and simmer gently for about 20 minutes. Put the lid on for this but leave a little gap (so it's not quite on) because, with the presence of the milk, it could boil over. Keep a close eye on it anyway.

While that's happening, pre-heat the grill to its highest setting for 10 minutes. Mix the rest of the sweetcorn with the melted butter, spread it out on a baking tray, season with salt and pepper and pop it under the hot grill about 3 inches (7.5 cm) from the heat – it will take about 8 minutes to become nicely toasted and golden, but remember to move the sweetcorn around on the baking tray halfway through.

When the soup is ready, leave it to cool a little, then pour it into a food processor or blender and blend it to a purée, leaving a little bit of texture – it doesn't need to be absolutely smooth. You will probably need to do this in two batches, in which case you'll need to have a large bowl handy to put the first batch into. Serve the soup in warm bowls with the toasted sweetcorn sprinkled over.

Mussel and Saffron Soup
Serves 4

2 lb 4 oz (1 kg) fresh mussels

2 good pinches of saffron stamens

15 fl oz (425 ml) dry white wine

2 oz (50 g) butter

4 shallots, finely chopped

1 large clove garlic, finely chopped

1 oz (25 g) plain flour

8 fl oz (225 ml) milk

7 fl oz (200 ml) crème fraîche

3 tablespoons very finely chopped
fresh chives

salt and freshly milled
white pepper

This is a smart soup, great if you're entertaining, and now that the mussels come with much of the cleaning and scrubbing already done, it isn't half the bother it used to be.

First of all, you need to prepare the mussels so begin by discarding any that have broken shells or any that don't close when given a sharp tap with a knife. Then, under cold running water, scrub the mussels, removing any barnacles, and pull out the little hairy 'beards'. After you have cleaned each mussel, place it straight into a bowl of clean water and when they're all in, swirl them around to get rid of any lingering bits of grit or sand. Drain them into a colander and they are now ready to be cooked. Next, pour the wine into a large, wide-bottomed pan and when the wine comes to the boil, put two tablespoonfuls into a cup or small bowl. Stir in the saffron and leave it to infuse. Next, tip the mussels into the pan, cover with a lid and leave on a high heat for 4-5 minutes. Have ready a colander lined with fine muslin or a clean, fine tea towel, set over a large bowl, and when the mussels are ready, tip them into the colander and leave them to drain. Now rinse out the pan (in case there is any fine grit left from the mussels) and melt the butter in it and then, over a low heat, soften the chopped shallots in the melted butter for about 5 minutes or until lightly golden.

Meanwhile, remove the mussels from the shells, discarding the shells as you go, and make sure you throw away any mussels that have not opened during cooking. Now tip the reserved mussel cooking liquid into a jug. Next, add the garlic to the softened shallots and cook for a further 30 seconds, follow that with the flour and, using a small pointed wooden spoon, stir quite vigorously to make a smooth, glossy paste. Now increase the heat to medium and begin to add the reserved mussel cooking liquid, a little at a time, still stirring. When all the liquid has been added, bring the mixture up to simmering point and cook on the lowest possible heat for 1 minute, stirring all the time. Next, add the saffron (and its soaking liquid), the milk and the crème fraîche. Bring the soup back up to a gentle simmer, switch to a balloon whisk and whisk until you have a smooth, creamy mixture. Now add the shelled mussels, two tablespoons of chives and heat gently for 5 minutes. Season and serve in warmed bowls, garnished with the remaining chopped chives.

Carrot and Artichoke Soup
Serves 6-8

1 lb (450 g) carrots

1 lb 8 oz (700 g) Jerusalem artichokes

3 oz (75 g) butter

1 medium onion, roughly chopped

3 celery stalks, trimmed and chopped

2½ pints (1.5 litres) vegetable stock

salt and freshly milled black pepper

To garnish

6-8 teaspoons crème fraîche

fresh flat-leaf parsley leaves

I love serving this, one of my most favourite soups. First, it has an extremely rich, beautiful colour, almost saffron-like, I would say. And second, people can never quite guess what it is. Jerusalem artichokes don't look user-friendly, but once you've cut off and discarded all the knobbly bits, the flavour is quite outstanding.

Start by peeling and de-knobbling the artichokes and, as you peel them, cut them into rough chunks and place them in a bowl of cold, salted water to prevent them from discolouring. Then scrape the carrots and slice them into largish chunks.

Now melt the butter in a large saucepan and soften the onion and celery in it for 5 minutes, keeping the heat fairly low. Next, drain the artichokes and add them to the pan, along with the carrots. Add some salt and, keeping the heat very low, put a lid on and let the vegetables sweat for 10 minutes to release their juices.

After that, pour in the stock, stir well, put the lid back on and simmer, very gently, for a further 20 minutes, or until the vegetables are soft. Now cool the soup slightly, then liquidise it in two batches – a large bowl is useful here to put the first batch in. Then return the soup to the pan, taste to check the seasoning and re-heat very gently until it just comes to simmering point. Serve in hot soup bowls, each garnished with a swirl of crème fraîche and a few parsley leaves.

Black Bean Soup with Black Bean Salsa
Serves 4

9 oz (250 g) dried black beans

2 tablespoons olive oil

3 oz (75 g) smoked bacon,
or pancetta, derinded and finely
chopped

1 large onion, chopped small

1 fat clove garlic, crushed

2 oz (50 g) each carrot and swede,
peeled and chopped small

½ oz (10 g) fresh coriander, stalks
finely chopped (leaves reserved for
the salsa)

1 teaspoon cumin seeds

1 teaspoon Tabasco sauce

2 pints (1.2 litres) chicken stock

juice of ½ lime (reserve remaining
half for the salsa)

1 heaped tablespoon crème fraîche

salt and freshly milled
black pepper

For the salsa

3 tablespoons cooked beans
(see method)

2 large tomatoes (not too ripe),
skinned

1 small red onion, finely chopped

1 green chilli, deseeded and
chopped

reserved coriander leaves

1 dessertspoon extra virgin olive oil

reserved juice of ½ lime
(see above)

salt and freshly milled
black pepper

This soup is stunning and one you'll want to make over and over again. If you forget to soak the beans overnight, bring them up to the boil for 10 minutes, then pre-soak them for two hours. If you're entertaining and want to have some fun, serve this soup, mixed together – half and half – with Tuscan White Bean Soup (see picture opposite and page 81).

It's best to start the soup the night before by throwing the beans into a large pan (6 pint/3.5 litre capacity) and covering them with about twice their volume of cold water. Next day, drain them in a colander and rinse them under a cold running tap. Now take the saucepan and heat the olive oil. As soon as it's really hot, add the chopped bacon, or pancetta, and cook for about 5 minutes. Then turn the heat down to medium, stir in the onion, garlic, carrot, swede and coriander stalks and continue to cook for another 10 minutes with the lid on, stirring everything round once or twice.

While that's happening, heat a small frying pan over a medium heat, then add the cumin seeds and dry-roast them for about 1 minute until they become aromatic and start to dance in the pan. Now crush them to a coarse powder with a pestle and mortar. Add this to the vegetables, along with the drained beans, Tabasco sauce and stock (but no salt at this stage), then bring everything up to a gentle simmer for about 1½ hours with the lid on. When the time is up, use a slotted spoon to remove 3 tablespoons of the beans, rinse and drain them in a sieve and reserve them for the salsa. Now let the soup cool a little, then purée it. The best way to do this is in batches in a blender with a bowl to hand to put the first batch in. Now return the soup to the saucepan, add the lime juice, season with salt and pepper and it's ready for re-heating. To make the salsa, cut the skinned tomatoes in half and gently squeeze each half in your hand to remove the seeds, then chop the tomato into small dice and place it in a bowl, along with the reserved beans, the red onion, chilli, reserved coriander leaves and the extra virgin olive oil. Then add the juice of half a lime, some salt and freshly milled black pepper and leave it aside for the flavours to mingle and be absorbed for about 1 hour. To serve the soup, re-heat it very gently, being careful not to allow it to come to the boil, as this will spoil the flavour of the soup. Serve in warm soup bowls, adding a spoonful of crème fraîche and an equal portion of salsa sprinkled over the surface.

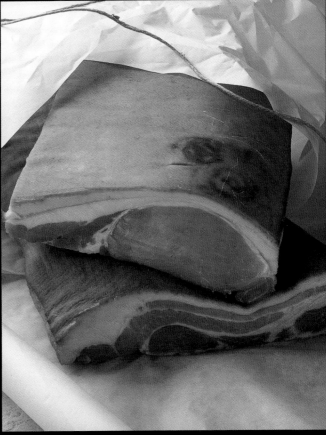

Wild Mushroom and Walnut Soup
Serves 8

1 oz (25 g) dried porcini mushrooms

2 oz (50 g) butter

4 oz (110 g) open-cap mushrooms, chopped

2 medium carrots, peeled and chopped

2 celery stalks, chopped

1 medium onion, chopped

1 leek, washed and chopped

2 bay leaves

1 teaspoon chopped fresh thyme

½ teaspoon chopped fresh sage

2 cloves garlic, crushed

salt

To finish

8 oz (225 g) small open-cap mushrooms – keep 4 whole and chop the rest finely

4 oz (110 g) walnuts, ground in a nut mill or food processor

1 oz (25 g) butter

3 fl oz (75 ml) single cream, plus a little extra, to serve

3 fl oz (75 ml) dry sherry

1 dessertspoon lemon juice

salt and freshly milled black pepper

Walnuts, together with some dried wild porcini mushrooms, can be used to make an unusual and special soup for a dinner party, warming lunch or supper snack, with some good bread and cheese to follow.

First, place the dried mushrooms in a jug with 10 fl oz (275 ml) boiling water and leave them to soak for 30 minutes. Meanwhile, in a very large saucepan melt the 2 oz (50 g) butter, then add the open-cap mushrooms, carrots, celery, onion, leek and herbs and garlic, stir well over a gentle heat until everything is glistening with a coating of butter, then pour in the dried mushrooms and their soaking water, followed by 3½ pints (2 litres) hot water. Add some salt, then bring up to a gentle simmer and, keeping the heat low, let the soup barely simmer for 1 hour.

After that, place a colander over a large bowl and strain the soup into it. Remove the bay leaves, and purée the vegetables with a little bit of the stock in a liquidiser or processor, then return this to the rest of the stock and whisk to a smooth consistency. To finish, return the saucepan to the heat with the 1 oz (25 g) butter. Lightly sauté the chopped mushrooms for about 5 minutes. After that, pour in the soup mixture, stir in the ground walnuts, season with salt and pepper, and let it continue cooking gently for 10 minutes. While that's happening, use your sharpest knife to slice the 4 reserved whole mushrooms into wafer-thin slices for a garnish.

When you are ready to serve the soup, stir in the cream, sherry and lemon juice and serve piping hot with a swirl of cream and the slices of raw mushroom floating on top.

Cauliflower Soup with Roquefort
Serves 4-6

1 medium, good-sized cauliflower
(about 1 lb 4 oz/570 g)

2 oz (50 g) Roquefort, crumbled
into small pieces

2 bay leaves

1 oz (25 g) butter

1 medium onion, chopped

2 sticks celery, chopped

1 large leek, trimmed, washed
and chopped

4 oz (110 g) potato, peeled and
chopped into dice

2 tablespoons half-fat crème
fraîche, plus a little extra to serve

1 tablespoon snipped fresh chives,
to garnish

salt and freshly milled
black pepper

This is a truly sublime soup, as the cauliflower and Roquefort seem to meld together so well, but I have also tried it with mature Cheddar, and I'm sure it would be good with any cheese you happen to have handy. More good news – it takes little more than 40 minutes to make.

The stock for this is very simply made with all the cauliflower trimmings. All you do is trim the cauliflower into small florets and then take the stalk bits, including the green stems, and place these trimmings in a medium saucepan. Then add 2½ pints (1.5 litres) of water, the bay leaves and some salt, bring it up to the boil and simmer for 20 minutes with a lid.

Meanwhile, take another large saucepan with a well-fitting lid, melt the butter in it over a gentle heat, then add the onion, celery, leek and potato, cover and let the vegetables gently sweat for 15 minutes. Keep the heat very low, then, when the stock is ready, strain it into the pan to join the vegetables, adding the bay leaves as well, but throwing out the rest. Now add the cauliflower florets, bring it all back up to simmering point and simmer very gently for 20-25 minutes, until the cauliflower is completely tender, this time without a lid.

After that, remove the bay leaves and leave the soup to cool a little, then place the contents of the saucepan into a food processor or blender and process until the soup is smooth and creamy. If you need to do this in batches, pour the first batch into a bowl while you whiz the second batch. Next, return the soup to the saucepan, stir in the crème fraîche and cheese and keep stirring until the cheese has melted and the soup is hot but not boiling. Check the seasoning, then serve in hot bowls, garnished with a little more crème fraîche, if you like, and the chives.

Tomato, Apple and Celery Cream Soup
Serves 4

5-6 oz (150-175 g) tomatoes, quartered – use the stalks as well

5-6 oz (150-175 g) apples, quartered – use the cores as well

5-6 oz (150-175 g) celery, cut into 2 inch (5 cm) lengths, plus leaves

2 oz (50 g) butter

4 oz (110 g) onions, finely chopped

2 fl oz (55 ml) dry sherry

freshly grated nutmeg

1 small pinch of ground ginger

¼ teaspoon salt

freshly milled black pepper

1 pint (570 ml) chicken or vegetable stock

apple slices and snipped fresh chives, to garnish

croutons, to serve (see page 129)

This is one of cookery writer John Tovey's famous soups and it demonstrates his own method of sweating vegetables for quite a long initial cooking, sealed with greaseproof paper. This really brings out all the flavour.

First, melt the butter in a large, heavy pan, then add the onions and cook gently until golden (about 10 minutes), taking care that they don't burn or catch on the bottom. Add the sherry, vegetables, fruit, spices and seasoning to the pan, place a double thickness of greaseproof paper (well dampened with cold water) over the ingredients, and cover the pan with a lid.

Simmer very gently for 1 hour, checking from time to time that nothing is sticking. After that, add the stock to the contents of the pan (first removing the paper!), and stir everything. Now slightly cool the soup and transfer it – in two batches – to a liquidiser to blend it, then press through a sieve (to remove pips and stalks) and return it to a clean pan. Re-heat, check the seasoning, ladle into warmed soup bowls, and garnish each serving with an apple slice and some snipped chives. Serve with croutons.

Tuscan White Bean Soup
with Frizzled Shallots and Pancetta
Serves 4

8 oz (225 g) dried cannellini beans

4 tablespoons extra virgin olive oil

1 large onion, chopped

2 fat cloves garlic, crushed

1 stalk celery, trimmed and chopped

1 good sprig each of parsley, thyme and rosemary

1 bay leaf

2 pints (1.2 litres) chicken stock

juice of ½ lemon

salt and freshly milled black pepper

For the frizzled shallots and pancetta garnish

4 shallots, finely sliced into rings

3 oz (75 g) thinly sliced pancetta or streaky bacon

3 tablespoons olive oil

If you look down the list of ingredients here you might be forgiven for thinking this doesn't sound very exciting. Yet Italian cannellini beans transformed into a soup are just wonderful, both in texture and in flavour. This is nice served with the Black Bean Soup with Black Bean Salsa (see page 70). If you want to make the garnish in advance you can re-frizzle both in a hot frying pan just before serving.

First of all, you need to soak the beans in twice their volume of cold water overnight or, failing that, use the same amount of cold water, bring them up to the boil, boil for 10 minutes and leave them to soak for 2 hours. When you're ready to make the soup, heat 2 tablespoons of the olive oil in a large (6 pint/3.5 litre) saucepan and gently soften the onion in it for 5 minutes. Then add the garlic and continue to cook gently for about 1 minute. After that, add the drained beans, celery, herbs, bay leaf and black pepper, but no salt at this stage. Now pour in the stock and stir well. As soon as it reaches a gentle simmer, put a lid on and keep it at the gentlest simmer for 1½ hours, stirring it from time to time. When the time is up, check the beans are tender and, if not, continue to cook them for a further 15-30 minutes. When the beans are ready, season with salt, leave to cool a little, then liquidise them in two batches (pour the first batch into a bowl while you blend the second lot of beans). When you are ready to serve the soup, re-heat it gently without letting it come to the boil, then add the lemon juice, check the seasoning and add 2 more tablespoons of olive oil just before serving.

While you're re-heating the soup, make the garnish: roll the pancetta or bacon strips into a cigar shape, then with a sharp knife cut them into fine shreds, which you then need to separate out. Now heat 2 tablespoons of the oil in a large frying pan over a high heat, and when it is hot and shimmering, fry the shallots for 3-4 minutes, stirring occasionally so they don't catch on the base of the pan. When they are crisp and golden brown, lift them on to crumpled kitchen paper to drain, using a draining spoon. Now heat another tablespoon of oil in the same pan and fry the pancetta or bacon over a high heat for about 2 minutes until they, too, are golden and crunchy. Drain on kitchen paper, then serve the shallots and pancetta on the soup as it goes to the table.

Libyan Soup with Couscous
Serves 6

6 oz (175 g) finely chopped raw lamb, leg steak or similar

2 oz (50 g) couscous

1 heaped teaspoon coriander seeds

1 heaped teaspoon cumin seeds

2 tablespoons groundnut or other flavourless oil

1 large onion, chopped

2 cloves garlic, crushed with 1 teaspoon sea salt in a pestle and mortar

1 heaped teaspoon ground allspice

2 heaped teaspoons mild chilli powder

5 oz (150 g) tomato purée

1 green chilli, deseeded and chopped

2 teaspoons caster sugar

1 pint (570 ml) good lamb stock

4 oz (110 g) dried chickpeas (soaked overnight in twice their volume of cold water)

1 tablespoon chopped fresh parsley

1 tablespoon chopped fresh mint

salt, to taste

To serve

lemon wedges

pitta bread

This recipe first appeared in *The Food Aid Cookery Book*, published in 1986, and was contributed by Mary El-Rayes. It's a truly wonderful soup, meaty with lots of fragrant flavour, and perfect for serving on a really cold day with pitta bread warm from the oven.

Begin by pre-heating a small frying pan over a medium heat, then add the coriander and cumin seeds and dry-roast them for about 2-3 minutes, moving them around the pan until they change colour and begin to dance. This will draw out their full spicy flavour. Now crush them quite finely with a pestle and mortar.

Next, heat 1 tablespoon of the oil in a large (6 pint/3.5 litre) saucepan and gently cook the onion until soft and lightly browned, for about 5 or 6 minutes, then add the crushed garlic and sea salt and let that cook for another 2 minutes. After that, add the crushed seeds, the allspice and chilli powder and stir them into the juices in the pan. Now transfer all this to a plate and keep it aside while you heat the other tablespoon of oil in the same pan until it's very hot. Then add the pieces of lamb and brown them, quickly turning them over and keeping them on the move.

Turn the heat down and now return the onion and spice mixture to the pan to join the meat, adding the tomato purée, chopped chilli and caster sugar. Stir everything together, then add the stock and 1½ pints (850 ml) water. Give it all another good stir then drain the soaked chickpeas, discarding their soaking liquid, and add these to the pan. Give a final stir, then put a lid on and simmer as gently as possible for 1 hour or until the chickpeas are tender.

When you're ready to serve the soup, taste it, add some salt, then add the couscous, parsley and mint and take the pan off the heat. Put the lid back on and let it stand for 3 minutes before serving in hot soup bowls. Serve with lemon wedges to squeeze into the soup and some warm pitta bread.

Eliza Acton's Vegetable Mulligatawny
Serves 8

3 large onions, chopped

1 lb 8 oz (700 g) peeled marrow or unpeeled courgettes, cut into 1 inch (2.5 cm) cubes

1 large potato, peeled and cut into 1 inch (2.5 cm) cubes

8 oz (225 g) tomatoes, skinned and chopped

4 oz (110 g) butter

3 whole cardamom pods, seeds only

1 teaspoon each cumin and fennel seeds

1 dessertspoon coriander seeds

3 fl oz (75 ml) white basmati rice, cooked in 6 fl oz (175 ml) boiling water

1½ pints (850 ml) hot vegetable stock

small croutons, to serve (see page 129)

salt and freshly milled black pepper

Eliza Acton is one of my favourite cookery writers and this is a recipe that I adapted from her cookery book, which was published in 1840.

First, melt the butter in a large (6 pint/3.5 litre) saucepan, then add the onions and cook until they're a golden brown colour. Now place the cardamom, cumin, fennel and coriander seeds in a small frying pan to dry-roast – this will take 2-3 minutes. As soon as the seeds start to jump, tip them into a mortar and crush them finely, then add them to the onions.

Now add the marrow or courgettes, potato and tomatoes. Season well, then let the vegetables cook gently, covered, until soft – about 20 minutes.

Next, when the vegetables have cooled a little, put them into a blender and reduce to a purée. You will need to do this in more than one batch, so a large bowl to put each batch in is helpful here. Then pour the purée back into the saucepan and stir in the cooked rice, together with the stock. Re-heat gently, cook for about 5 minutes more, then serve with some crisp croutons sprinkled in each bowl.

Curried Parsnip and Apple Soup with Parsnip Crisps
Serves 6

1 lb 8 oz (700 g) young parsnips

1 medium Bramley apple
(6 oz/175 g)

1 heaped teaspoon coriander
seeds

1 heaped teaspoon cumin seeds

6 whole cardamom pods
(seeds only)

1½ oz (40 g) butter

1 tablespoon groundnut or other
flavourless oil

2 medium onions, chopped

2 cloves garlic, chopped

1 heaped teaspoon turmeric

1 heaped teaspoon ground ginger

2 pints (1.2 litres) good-flavoured
vegetable or chicken stock

salt and freshly milled
black pepper

For the parsnip crisps

1 medium to large parsnip
(10-12 oz/275-350 g)

6 tablespoons groundnut or other
flavourless oil

salt

This is such a lovely soup. The sweetness of the parsnips is sharpened by the presence of the apple, and the subtle flavour of the spices comes through beautifully. If you like, you can make these in advance, as they will stay crisp for a couple of hours.

Begin by heating a small frying pan and dry-roasting the coriander, cumin and cardamom seeds – this is to toast them and draw out their flavour. After 2-3 minutes they will change colour and start to jump in the pan. Remove them from the pan and crush them finely with a pestle and mortar. Next, heat the butter and oil in a large (6 pint/3.5 litre) saucepan until the butter begins to foam, then add the onions and gently soften for about 5 minutes before adding the garlic. Let that cook, along with the onions, for another 2 minutes, then add all the crushed spices, along with the turmeric and ginger.

Now stir and let it all continue to cook gently for a few more minutes while you peel and chop the parsnips into 1 inch (2.5 cm) dice. Add the parsnips to the saucepan, stirring well, then pour in the stock, add some seasoning and let the soup simmer as gently as possible for 1 hour without putting on a lid.

To make the parsnip crisps, peel the parsnip and then slice it into rounds as thinly as you possibly can, using a sharp knife, or even better, a mandoline. Now heat the oil in a 10 inch (25.5 cm) frying pan until it is very hot, almost smoking, then fry the parsnip slices in batches until they are golden brown, for about 2-3 minutes (they will not stay flat or colour evenly but will twist into lovely shapes). As they're cooked, remove them with a slotted spoon and spread them out on kitchen paper to drain. Sprinkle lightly with salt.

When the soup has been simmering for an hour, remove it from the heat, cool it slightly, then liquidise it in a blender, if possible. If not, use a food processor and then a sieve. Either way, if you need to purée it in batches, put the first batch in a bowl while you do the second. Now return it to the saucepan, taste to check the seasoning, then, when you're ready to serve, re-heat very gently. While that's happening, peel the apple and, as the soup just reaches simmering point, grate the apple into it. Be careful to let the soup barely simmer for only 3-4 minutes. Serve in hot soup bowls, garnished with the parsnip crisps.

Roasted Pumpkin Soup with Melting Cheese
Serves 6

3-3 lb 8 oz (1.35-1.6 kg) pumpkin

1 tablespoon groundnut or other flavourless oil

1 oz (25 g) butter

1 large onion, finely chopped

1½ pints (850 ml) vegetable or chicken stock

15 fl oz (425 ml) whole milk

freshly grated nutmeg

salt and freshly milled black pepper

To serve

4 oz (110 g) Gruyère or Fontina, cut into ¼ inch (5 mm) dice

2 oz (50 g) Gruyère or Fontina, coarsely grated

2 tablespoons crème fraîche

croutons (see page 129) and chopped fresh flat-leaf parsley

Pre-heat the oven to gas mark 9, 475°F (240°C).

The lovely thing about pumpkin is that it has a really velvety texture in soup, and if it's oven-roasted before you add it to the soup, it gives an unusual nuttiness to the flavour. Just before serving, add little cubes of quick melting cheese, such as Gruyère, or, if you're lucky enough to get it, Fontina. Then finding little bits of half-melted cheese in the soup that stretch up on the spoon is an absolute delight.

Begin by cutting the pumpkin in half through the stalk, then cut each half into four again and scoop out the seeds, using a large spoon. Then brush the surface of each section with the oil and place them on a solid baking sheet. Season with salt and pepper, then pop them on a high shelf of the oven to roast for 25-30 minutes or until tender when tested with a skewer.

Meanwhile, melt the butter in a large (6 pint/3.5 litre) saucepan over a high heat, add the onion, stir it round and when it begins to colour around the edges, after about 5 minutes, turn the heat down. Let it cook very gently without a lid, giving it a stir from time to time, for about 20 minutes.

Then remove the pumpkin from the oven and leave it aside to cool. Now add the stock and the milk to the onion, and leave them with the heat turned low to slowly come up to simmering point. Next, scoop out the flesh of the pumpkin with a sharp knife and add it to the stock, together with a seasoning of salt, pepper and nutmeg. Then let it all simmer very gently for about 15-20 minutes.

Next, the soup should be cooled a little, then processed to a purée. Because there's a large volume of soup, it's best to do this in two halves, putting the first half in a bowl as you go. Whiz the soup until it's smoothly blended, but, as an extra precaution, it's best to pass it through a sieve as well, in case there are any unblended fibrous bits. Taste and season well, then when you're ready to serve the soup, re-heat it gently just up to simmering point, being careful not to let it boil.

Finally, stir in the diced cheese, then ladle the soup into warm soup bowls. Garnish each bowl with a teaspoonful of crème fraîche and scatter with the grated cheese, a few croutons as well, if you like them, and a sprinkling of parsley.

Slow-cooked Celery and Celeriac Soup
Serves 6

1 lb (450 g) celery stalks and a few leaves reserved

1 lb 4 oz (570 g) celeriac

1 medium onion

2½ pints (1.5 litres) hot vegetable stock

3 bay leaves

salt and freshly milled black pepper

To garnish

2 tablespoons natural yoghurt or crème fraîche

2 teaspoons celery salt

reserved celery leaves (see above)

Pre-heat the oven to gas mark 1, 275°F (140°C).

Here, because the vegetables are very slowly cooked, this soup has lots of subtle flavours of combined celery and celeriac – is perfect for a low fat diet – and is very satisfying and filling, especially served with bread.

Just a word first about preparing the vegetables. You need to use a potato peeler to pare off any really stringy bits from the outside stalks of the celery. The nice thing is that the outside stalks are fine for soups – so if you're using a whole head of celery, once you've weighed out the amount you need, you can keep the tender inside stalks for munching on.

Peeling the celeriac may mean you lose quite a bit of the outside, as it's very fibrous. Once that's done, weigh it (you need 1 lb/450 g) and cut it into large chunks. The celery should also be cut into large chunks, and the same with the onion. All you do now is pop the whole lot into a 6 pint (3.5 litre), lidded, flameproof casserole. Then add the stock and bay leaves, along with some salt and freshly milled black pepper. Bring it all up to simmering point on the hob, then put the lid on and transfer it to the oven to simmer very gently and slowly for 3 hours. After that, remove the bay leaves, allow the soup to cool a little, then blend in batches until smooth. A large bowl to put each batch in is helpful here.

Now return the soup to the casserole and bring it back to a gentle simmer, tasting to check the seasoning before serving. Serve in hot bowls with the yoghurt or crème fraîche spooned on top and the celery salt sprinkled over, garnished with a few celery leaves.

Winter

Celery Soup with Nutmeg
Serves 4

12 oz (350 g) celery stalks, trimmed and chopped, leaves reserved

1 oz (25 g) butter

4 oz (110 g), potatoes, peeled and cut into chunks

the white parts of 2 medium leeks, trimmed, washed and sliced

1 pint (570 ml) vegetable or chicken stock

10 fl oz (275 ml) milk

¼ teaspoon celery seeds

2 tablespoons double cream or crème fraîche

a good grating of fresh nutmeg

salt and freshly milled black pepper

This recipe has the purest of flavour and is light and creamy. I like to make it when there has been a light frost when the celery is sweetest of all and the flavour is exceptional.

In a largish pan, melt the butter over a low heat. Then add the celery to the pan with the potatoes and prepared leeks. Then stir to coat the vegetables with butter, cover and cook very gently for about 15 minutes, shaking the pan from time to time to prevent the vegetables from sticking.

Next, pour in the stock and milk and sprinkle in the celery seeds and some salt. Bring the soup to simmering point, then cover once more and cook over a very low heat for 20-25 minutes or until the vegetables are really tender. Leave the soup to cool a little, then liquidise, blending it in batches (have a bowl handy for the first batch). Now return the purée to the pan and add the cream or crème fraîche and the nutmeg. Bring the soup back to the boil, check the seasoning, adding more salt and some pepper, if necessary. Then just before serving, chop the reserved celery leaves and stir them into the soup to give it extra colour.

Chestnut Soup
with Bacon and Thyme Croutons
Serves 4

7 oz (200 g) cooked and peeled whole chestnuts

1 stick of celery, trimmed and chopped

1 small onion, chopped

1 small carrot, peeled and chopped

2 pints (1.2 litres) ham or vegetable stock

salt and freshly milled black pepper

For the croutons

1 rasher bacon, derinded and very finely chopped

½ teaspoon finely chopped fresh thyme leaves

4 oz (110 g) stale white bread, cut into small cubes

4 tablespoons olive oil

A bone from a baked ham makes a good stock for this one – but if you use vegetable stock, it is still an excellent soup. You can buy the chestnuts ready peeled and vacuum-packed in supermarkets and specialist food shops.

To make the soup, you simply place all the ingredients in a large saucepan, season lightly with salt and pepper, bring up to simmering point, then put a lid on and simmer very gently for 45 minutes.

While that's happening, you can prepare the croutons. Heat the oil in a large frying pan and cook the bacon gently for 5 minutes, then turn the heat up to its highest setting, add the cubes of bread, together with the thyme, and toss them around (keeping them constantly on the move) until they, and the bacon, have turned a deep golden brown colour and become very crisp and crunchy. Turn them out on to some absorbent kitchen paper.

Then, as soon as the soup is ready, allow it to cool slightly, then transfer it to a blender and purée until smooth. You may need to do this in more than one batch, in which case, it is a good idea to have a bowl to put the soup in as it is ready. Re-heat the soup in the pan, season to taste and serve in warmed soup bowls, with the croutons, bacon and thyme sprinkled over.

La Potée
(French farmhouse soup with bacon, sausage and beans)
Serves 8

6 oz (175 g) dried haricot beans

2 lb (900 g) unsmoked gammon joint

4 Toulouse or coarse-textured, herb-flavoured, pork sausages

a few parsley stalks

a sprig of thyme

2 tablespoons groundnut or other flavourless oil

1 fat clove garlic, crushed

2 medium leeks, trimmed, cleaned and sliced into ¼ inch (5 mm) rings

2 medium carrots, peeled and sliced into ¼ inch (5 mm) slices

1 turnip or 4 oz (110 g) swede, peeled and cut into ½ inch (1 cm) chunks

1 celery stalk, trimmed and chopped

2 medium potatoes (8 oz/225 g), peeled and cut into ½ inch (1 cm) chunks

1 small onion, chopped

6 oz (175 g) trimmed Savoy or other cabbage, finely shredded

salt and freshly milled black pepper

To garnish

chopped fresh parsley

extra virgin olive oil

You will also need a very large saucepan with a capacity of about 10 pints (5.75 litres).

This is a traditional French farmhouse soup or *potée* that is really a sort of cross between a soup and a stew and makes a meal in itself. If you have a ridged griddle, it's nice to serve chargrilled French country bread or, failing that, some warm sourdough bread.

First of all, you need to soak the beans, so either put them into a bowl and cover them with cold water to soak overnight or alternatively, put the beans into a saucepan, cover them with cold water and bring to the boil and boil for 10 minutes, then remove them from the heat and allow them to soak for 2 hours. Either way, once the beans are soaked, drain and reserve the soaking liquid.

Now make the soaking liquid up to 4 pints (2.25 litres) and place the gammon into the large pan with the soaked beans, parsley, thyme and the 4 pints (2.25 litres) of liquid. Bring to the boil, boil for 10 minutes (spooning off any scum as it appears), then cover and simmer the gammon over a low heat for 1½ hours. Meanwhile, in a frying pan, slowly brown the sausages in a tablespoon of the oil. When they're a nice brown colour all over, remove them to a plate and slice them into ¼ inch (5 mm) slices.

Next, when the gammon is ready, lift it out of the pan and on to a board. Then drain the rest of the ingredients from the pan into a colander, set over a large bowl, reserving the cooking liquor and beans but discarding the parsley and thyme stalks. Rinse out the pan and add the second tablespoon of oil to it. Heat the oil and now stir in the garlic and all the prepared vegetables, except the shredded cabbage. Then cover and cook the vegetables gently for about 15 minutes or until they are tender when tested with a skewer. Meanwhile, skin the gammon, remove all the excess fat and chop the meat into smallish, soup-size pieces. When the vegetables are ready, return the pieces of gammon, along with the beans, to the saucepan. Now add enough of the cooking liquor to give the whole thing a suitably soupy consistency – 2½-2¾ pints (1.5 -1.6 litres) - and season with plenty of freshly milled black pepper. Bring the soup back to the boil, then add the slices of sausage and the cabbage. Simmer for a further few minutes, uncovered, or until the cabbage has wilted, then ladle the piping hot soup into deep bowls and garnish each one with a scattering of chopped parsley and a drizzle of extra virgin olive oil.

Slow-cooked Jerusalem Artichoke and Leek Soup
Serves 6

1 lb (450 g) Jerusalem artichokes, trimmed

1 lb (450 g) leeks

1 small onion

2½ pints (1.5 litres) hot vegetable stock

3 bay leaves

salt and freshly milled black pepper

To garnish

2 tablespoons natural yoghurt

freshly snipped chives

Pre-heat the oven to gas mark 1, 275°F (140°C).

This soup has no fat at all in it and has a lovely pure vegetable flavour because it's given long, slow treatment. Serve it with a swirl of natural yoghurt and, if you like, a few snipped chives.

Start by peeling and de-knobbling the artichokes and, as you peel them, cut them into rough chunks and toss them into a bowl of cold salted water to prevent any discolouring. Now prepare the leeks. First, trim the tough green ends and throw them out, then make a vertical split about halfway down the centre of each leek and clean them by running them under the cold water tap while you fan out the layers – this will rid them of any hidden dust and grit. Then slice them in half lengthways and chop into large chunks and after that, peel the onion and cut that into large chunks too.

All you do now is pop the whole lot into a 6 pint (3.5 litre), lidded, flameproof casserole. Then add the stock and bay leaves, along with some salt and freshly milled black pepper. Bring it all up to simmering point on the hob, then put the lid on and transfer it to the oven to simmer very gently and slowly for 3 hours.

When the time is up, remove the bay leaves, allow the soup to cool a little, then blend in a liquidiser in batches until smooth. It is useful to have a large bowl handy to pour each batch into. Now return the puréed soup to the casserole and bring it back to a gentle simmer, tasting to check the seasoning before serving. Serve in hot bowls with the yoghurt swirled in and a few chives sprinkled on top.

French Onion Soup
Serves 6

1 lb 8 oz (700 g) onions,
thinly sliced

2 tablespoons olive oil

2 oz (50 g) butter

2 cloves garlic, crushed

½ teaspoon granulated sugar

2 pints (1.2 litres) good beef stock

10 fl oz (275 ml) dry white wine

2 tablespoons Cognac

salt and freshly milled
black pepper

For the croutons

French bread or baguettine, cut
into 1 inch (2.5 cm) diagonal slices

1 tablespoon olive oil

1-2 cloves garlic, crushed

To serve

6 large or 12 small croutons
(see above)

8 oz (225 g) Gruyère, grated

Pre-heat the oven to gas mark 4,
350°F (180°C).

There are few things more comforting than making a real French Onion Soup – slowly cooked, caramelised onions that turn mellow and sweet in a broth laced with white wine and Cognac. The whole thing is finished off with crunchy baked croutons of crusty bread topped with melted, toasted cheese. If ever there was a winter stomach warmer, this is surely it!

First make the croutons – begin by drizzling the olive oil on to a large, solid baking sheet, add the crushed garlic and then, using your hands, spread the oil and garlic all over the baking sheet. Now place the bread slices on top of the oil, then turn over each one so that both sides have been lightly coated with the oil. Bake them in the oven for 20-25 minutes till crispy and crunchy.

Next, place a large (6 pint/3.5 litre), heavy-based saucepan or flameproof casserole on a high heat and melt the oil and butter together. When this is very hot, add the onions, garlic and sugar, and keep turning them from time to time until the edges of the onions have turned dark – this will take about 6 minutes. Then reduce the heat to its lowest setting and leave the onions to carry on cooking very slowly for about 30 minutes, by which time the base of the pan will be covered with a rich, nut brown, caramelised film. After that, pour in the stock and white wine, season, then stir with a wooden spoon, scraping the base of the pan well. As soon as it all comes up to simmering point, turn down the heat to its lowest setting, then go away and leave it to cook very gently, without a lid, for about 1 hour.

All this can be done in advance but, when you're ready to serve the soup, bring it back up to simmering point, taste to check for seasoning – and if it's extra cold outside, add a couple of tablespoons of Cognac! Warm a tureen or soup bowls in a low oven and pre-heat the grill to its highest setting. Then ladle in the hot soup and top with the croutons, allowing them to float on the top of the soup.

Now sprinkle the grated Gruyère thickly over the croutons and place the whole lot under the grill until the cheese is golden brown and bubbling. Serve immediately – and don't forget to warn your guests that everything is very hot!

Butter Bean, Bacon and Parsley Soup
Serves 4

8 oz (225 g) dried butter beans

4 oz (110 g) smoked streaky bacon, derinded and chopped

3 tablespoons chopped fresh parsley, to serve

2 tablespoons groundnut or other flavourless oil

1 bay leaf

1 oz (25 g) butter

1 onion, finely chopped

1 leek, trimmed, cleaned and finely chopped

2 smallish celery stalks, finely chopped

1 large clove garlic, crushed

about 5 fl oz (150 ml) milk

salt and freshly milled black pepper

Butter beans, boiled on their own (as I remember them at school) tend to be dull, but they make a good, thick, creamy soup and have the great virtue of being able to absorb other flavours really well.

First of all, you need to soak the beans overnight in a pan by covering them with cold water, or, using the same amount of cold water, bring them up to the boil, boil for 10 minutes and leave them to soak for 2 hours. Either way, drain the beans.

Now heat 1 tablespoon of the oil in a medium saucepan and cook the bacon in it for 5 minutes or until lightly crispy and golden.

Next, add the bay leaf and 1¾ pints (1 litre) water to the pan with the drained beans. Bring to the boil, partially cover, and simmer gently for 20-30 minutes or until the beans are tender, skimming off any scum that appears on the surface. Meanwhile, heat the butter and remaining oil in a large saucepan and add the chopped onion, leek and celery. Stir to coat everything with butter and oil, and cook over a low heat for about 10 minutes.

Now tip the bacon, along with the cooked beans and their cooking liquor, into the pan containing the vegetables, discarding the bay leaf. Next, add the garlic, cover and continue simmering for a further 10 minutes or until the beans and vegetables are soft, then mash the beans against the sides of the pan with a large fork to thicken the soup. Now stir in the milk, season with salt and a generous grinding of freshly milled black pepper and stir everything together, before adding the chopped parsley to serve.

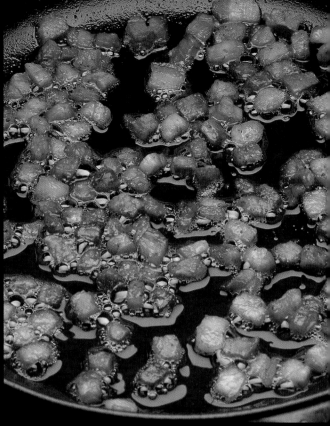

Puy Lentil Soup with Bacon
Serves 6

6 oz (175 g) Puy or green-brown lentils, rinsed

4 oz (110 g) smoked, streaky bacon or pancetta, derinded and finely chopped

1 tablespoon groundnut or other flavourless oil

2 carrots, peeled and finely chopped

2 medium onions, finely chopped

2 celery stalks, trimmed and finely sliced

8 oz (225 g) tinned Italian tomatoes

2 cloves garlic, crushed

3 pints (1.75 litres) vegetable stock

8 oz (225 g) cabbage, finely shredded

2 tablespoons chopped fresh parsley

salt and freshly milled black pepper

This is a very substantial soup, best made with the tiny French, greeny-black Puy lentils. If you can't get these, use green-brown lentils, which don't have the depth of flavour of the Puy lentils, but are still excellent and can be used in the same way.

Heat the oil in a large saucepan and fry the bacon or pancetta in it until the fat begins to run. Then stir in the prepared carrots, onions and celery and, with the heat fairly high, toss them around to brown them a little at the edges, stirring now and then.

Next, stir in the rinsed lentils, plus the tomatoes, followed by the crushed garlic, stir everything together, then pour in the stock.

As soon as the soup comes to the boil, put a lid on and simmer, as gently as possible, for about 30 minutes. Then add the cabbage and cook for 5 minutes or until the cabbage has wilted, taste and season with salt and plenty of freshly milled black pepper. Just before serving, stir in the chopped parsley.

Seafood and Coconut Laksa
Serves 4

24 raw tiger prawns

1 lb 2 oz (500 g) fresh mussels

4 oz (110 g) medium-thickness white rice noodles

14 fl oz (400 ml) tinned coconut milk

2 oz (50 g) shelled, unsalted macadamia nuts or peanuts

1 tablespoon groundnut or other flavourless oil

2 oz (50 g) piece of cucumber, peeled

4 oz (110 g) beansprouts

juice of 1 lime

a small bunch of fresh basil, stalks discarded and leaves roughly shredded

a small bunch of fresh mint, stalks discarded and leaves roughly shredded

sea salt

For the paste

3 medium red chillies, deseeded and chopped

1 dessertspoon dried shrimp paste

4 shallots, peeled

2 stems of lemon grass, trimmed and outer layer removed, stems chopped

small piece of fresh galangal or root ginger, peeled and roughly chopped

1 dessertspoon ground turmeric

This Malaysian-influenced recipe was given to me by Sarah Randell, the Editor of the Collection. She says you can make it using ready-made laksa paste but that it is infinitely better if you make it yourself.

First of all, you need to prepare the seafood. So, peel the prawns, then run the point of a small, sharp knife along the back of each one and remove any black threads that may be present. Now scrub the mussels under cold running water and remove any barnacles and pull off the little hairy 'beards'. Discard any mussels that are broken or don't close when given a sharp tap with a knife.

Now place the rice noodles in a bowl and cover with boiling water, then leave to soak for 10 minutes – they won't need any further cooking, just re-heating. Then drain the noodles in a colander when they are ready, rinse them in cold water and set aside.

Next, to make the paste, place all the paste ingredients, plus a tablespoon of water, into a blender or the bowl of a food processor and blend until smooth. Now place the macadamias or peanuts in a medium saucepan and dry-roast over a medium heat until golden brown, then remove to a plate. Add the oil to the same pan and, when warm, add the prepared paste and cook over a medium heat for 2 minutes. Add the coconut milk and stir, then leave to simmer gently for 10 minutes.

Meanwhile, cut the cucumber into four slices lengthways, then cut each into four long strips. Next, roughly chop the toasted nuts. When the coconut-milk mixture is ready, add the noodles, cucumber, three-quarters of the beansprouts and the lime juice. Now season with salt, to taste, then bring back to a simmer, add the prawns and mussels and cook for 3-5 minutes – the prawns should turn a pretty pink colour and all the mussels should open – discard any mussels that don't open during cooking. Now add half the shredded herbs, then mix the remaining herbs with the chopped nuts. Finally, ladle the laksa into four deep bowls, then sprinkle over the remaining beansprouts and the herb mixture.

Stilton Soup with Parmesan Croutons
Serves 4-6

4 oz (110 g) Stilton, grated

2 oz (50 g) butter

1 onion, finely chopped

1 leek, trimmed, cleaned
and chopped

1 large potato, peeled
and diced small

1 heaped tablespoon plain flour

5 fl oz (150 ml) dry cider

1 pint (570 ml) chicken stock

10 fl oz (275 ml) milk

1 tablespoon double cream

salt and freshly milled
black pepper

For the croutons

4 dessertspoons freshly grated
Parmesan

8 oz (225 g) stale bread, cut into
small cubes

4 tablespoons groundnut or other
flavourless oil

Not simply a recipe for leftover bits of Stilton (although useful for that) but a delicious, creamy soup that can enhance any supper party. It can obviously be made in advance, but be careful not to boil the soup when re-heating. The croutons also can be made well in advance and stored in an airtight container.

Start off by melting the butter in a thick-based saucepan, then add the prepared vegetables and some salt, and cook gently, with the lid on, for 5-10 minutes to draw out the juices. Next, stir in the flour to absorb the juices and, when they are smooth, gradually pour in the cider – still stirring. Now add the chicken stock, cover the pan and simmer gently for 30 minutes.

Meanwhile, make the croutons. Begin by pre-heating the oven to gas mark 4, 350°F (180°C), or pre-heat the grill. Then place the bread cubes in a bowl, sprinkle in the oil, then stir them around till the bread has soaked up all the oil. Next, add the freshly grated Parmesan, and stir again till all the bread cubes are well coated. Spread them out over a baking sheet and either bake in the pre-heated oven for 10 minutes, or else place them under the pre-heated grill, turning as necessary. If you use the grill, watch them like a hawk as they can burn very easily.

Once the 30 minutes are up, add the milk and Stilton to the saucepan and re-heat, stirring, until the cheese has melted and the soup is just below boiling point. Taste and season with salt and pepper, then stir in the cream and leave the soup to cool a bit. At this stage, you can purée it in a food processor or blender in batches (pour the first batch into a bowl while you purée the rest) – or, if you prefer the texture of the chopped vegetables, keep it as it is. Serve the soup with the Parmesan croutons.

Soup Flamande with Crème Fraîche and Frizzled Sprouts
Serves 4-6

12 oz (350 g) potatoes

2 large leeks, trimmed

12 oz (350 g) Brussels sprouts

2 oz (50 g) butter

15 fl oz (425 ml) vegetable stock

1 pint (570 ml) milk

2 rounded tablespoons crème fraîche

a squeeze of lemon juice

salt and freshly milled black pepper

For the garnish

4 tablespoons crème fraîche

4 large sprouts, trimmed and shredded

1 tablespoon olive oil

Sprouts heighten considerably in flavour after a hard frost and the large, fat, open-textured ones are too big for serving so they are just perfect for making this classic Flemish soup. So creamy and subtle is it that even determined sprout haters have been known to succumb to its charms. If you want to make the garnish in advance, you can re-frizzle the sprouts in a hot frying pan just before serving.

Start by peeling and thickly slicing the potatoes. Next, make a vertical split about halfway down the centre of each leek and clean them by running them under the cold water tap while you fan out the layers - this will rid them of any hidden dust and grit. Now slice them in half lengthways and chop into 1 inch (2.5 cm) pieces. Then trim the bases of the sprouts and discard any damaged outer leaves and quarter the larger sprouts and halve any smaller ones. Next, melt the butter in a good large saucepan, add the potatoes, leeks and sprouts, and stir well to coat them nicely in the butter. Add some salt and freshly milled black pepper, turn the heat to low, put a lid on and allow the vegetables to sweat gently for 5 minutes. Then add the stock and milk, bring everything up to simmering point and cook very gently for 20-25 minutes, or until the potatoes are soft. It's best to put the lid just three-quarters on to prevent the milk from boiling over and keep the heat really low.

After that, cool the soup and liquidise it in a blender or food processor in batches (it's helpful to have a bowl nearby to keep the first batch in), then return it to the pan. Add the 2 rounded tablespoons of crème fraîche, then re-heat the soup gently, taste and add a good squeeze of lemon juice and more seasoning, if it needs it.

Meanwhile, make the garnish while the soup is re-heating. To do this, heat the olive oil in a small frying pan over a high heat, and when the oil is really hot and shimmering, add the shredded sprouts and fry them, stirring occasionally, so they don't catch on the base of the pan. When they are crisp and golden brown – which should take 2-3 minutes – lift them, using a draining spoon, on to crumpled kitchen paper to drain. Serve the soup in hot bowls with a little crème fraîche spooned on top of each one and garnished with the frizzled sprouts.

Slow-cooked Root Vegetable Soup
Serves 6

8 oz (225 g) peeled carrots, cut into 2 inch (5 cm) lengths

8 oz (225 g) peeled celeriac, cut into 2 inch (5 cm) pieces

8 oz (225 g) trimmed and washed leeks, halved and cut into 2 inch (5 cm) lengths

8 oz (225 g) peeled swede, cut into 2 inch (5 cm) pieces

1 small onion, roughly chopped

2½ pints (1.5 litres) vegetable stock

3 bay leaves

salt and freshly milled black pepper

To serve

2 tablespoons fat-free Greek yoghurt

a few fresh chives, snipped

Pre-heat the oven to gas mark 1, 275°F (140°C).

Something happens to root vegetables when they're cooked very slowly for a long time: their flavour becomes mellow but at the same time more intense, and your kitchen is filled with aromas of goodness. This soup is also completely fat free.

There's not much to do here once everything is peeled and chopped. All you do is place everything in a large (6 pint/3.5 litre), lidded, flameproof casserole with a seasoning of salt and freshly milled pepper and bring it up to a gentle simmer, then put the lid on, place it in the lowest part of the oven and leave it there for 3 hours, by which time the vegetables will be meltingly tender. Now leave the soup to cool for a while.

Next, remove the bay leaves and process or liquidise the soup in several batches to a purée (it's a good idea to have a bowl handy to put the batches in as they are ready), then gently re-heat, and serve the soup in bowls with a teaspoon of Greek yoghurt swirled into each and garnished with the fresh chives.

Polish Beetroot Soup with Black Rye Croutons
Serves 4-6

For the soup

2 lb 4 oz (1 kg) uncooked beetroot, whole, but with stalks removed

1 rounded tablespoon plain flour, mixed to a paste with 1½ oz (40 g) softened butter

5 fl oz (150 ml) soured cream

3 tablespoons lemon juice

salt and freshly milled black pepper

For the stock

1 dessertspoon groundnut or other flavourless oil

9 oz (250 g) belly or shoulder of pork, cut into cubes

2 medium carrots, peeled and cut into chunks

1 large onion, roughly chopped

1 bay leaf

a handful of parsley stalks

salt and freshly milled black pepper

For the croutons

4 oz (110 g) black rye (pumpernickel) bread, cut into small cubes

1 dessertspoon olive oil

Pre-heat the oven to gas mark 4, 350°F (180°C).

Beetroot lovers know of its earthy charm and delicious but distinctive flavour. It makes wonderful soup, this one is Polish and especially good. Although the soup is a dazzling colour, you won't want your hands to match it, so it's best to wear gloves when you handle it.

First of all, you need to make a stock: heat the oil in a large (6 pint/3.5 litre) saucepan and, when it's really hot, brown the pieces of pork, carrot and onion, in batches, keeping the heat high so they turn brownish-black at the edges. This is important because it gives the stock a good flavour. When you're happy with the colour, after about 6 minutes, add 3 pints (1.75 litres) water, the bay leaf and parsley stalks, followed by a good seasoning of salt and freshly milled pepper. As soon as it begins to simmer, turn the heat down and let it simmer very gently, without a lid, for 40 minutes. After that, strain it through a sieve into a bowl, throw out the stock ingredients and rinse the saucepan to use again.

While the stock is cooking, you can deal with the beetroot. Place it in another saucepan, add enough boiling water to just cover it, then add a pinch of salt. Put on a lid and simmer gently for 40 minutes or until tender when pierced with a skewer. After that, drain off the water, then cover the beetroot with cold water to cool it down. As soon as it's cool enough to handle, take off the skin. Now reserve 1 beetroot (about 4 oz/110 g) for the garnish and cut the rest into cubes. Next, transfer it to the saucepan in which you made the stock, add the stock, bring to simmering point, cover and simmer gently for 20 minutes. Meanwhile, to make the croutons, place the oil and rye bread cubes in a small bowl, stir them so that they get an even coating, then arrange on a baking tray. Bake on a high shelf in the oven for 10 minutes (do use a kitchen timer here). Then leave to cool.

Now, using a draining spoon, transfer half of the beetroot to a blender, add the flour and butter paste, then put the lid on, and as soon as the motor is running, add the stock from the pan, give it all a whiz and pour into a bowl. Now blend the other half of the beetroot with 3 fl oz (75 ml) of soured cream. Pour this back into the pan with the other beetroot mixture, add the lemon juice, check the seasoning and re-heat gently. Grate the reserved beetroot, then serve the soup in warmed soup bowls, swirl in the remaining soured cream and scatter the croutons and grated beetroot on top.

Goulash Soup with Dumplings
Serves 4-6

1 lb (450 g) braising steak

1–2 tablespoons olive oil

1 large onion, chopped small

1 tablespoon plain flour

2 tablespoons hot paprika,
plus a little extra for sprinkling

¼ teaspoon dried marjoram
(if available)

½ teaspoon caraway seeds

1 clove garlic, crushed

14 oz (400 g) tinned Italian
chopped tomatoes

2½ pints (1.5 litres) beef
or vegetable stock

1 teaspoon tomato purée

1 lb (450 g) potatoes, peeled and
cut into ½ inch (1 cm) cubes

1 green or red pepper, deseeded
and chopped

5 fl oz (150 ml) soured cream

salt and freshly milled
black pepper

For the dumplings

4 oz (110 g) self-raising flour,
plus a little extra for dusting

2 oz (50 g) shredded suet

salt and freshly milled
black pepper

You will also need a 6 pint
(3.5 litre) lidded, flameproof
casserole.

I've always loved the goulash flavours of beef, tomatoes and spicy paprika and this soup is certainly a great 'winter warmer'. In fact, it's a meal in a bowl so no need for a main course, just some bread and cheese to follow.

Begin by trimming and cutting the meat into ½ inch (1 cm) pieces. Then heat the oil in the casserole and fry the meat in batches over a high heat until well browned, removing it to a plate as it is ready. Now stir in the onion, adding a little extra oil if needed. Cook the onion over a medium heat for about 5 minutes or until it's lightly browned, stirring now and then. Then return the meat to the casserole and sprinkle in the flour, paprika, marjoram (if using), caraway seeds and garlic and season with salt. Stir well and cook for a minute before adding the tomatoes and stock. When it comes to simmering point, cover and continue simmering very gently for 45 minutes.

After that, take the lid off and stir in the tomato purée, followed by the potatoes and chopped pepper, then bring the goulash back to a simmer and cook gently, covered, for 10 minutes, stirring occasionally.

Then, to make the dumplings, mix the flour and shredded suet in a bowl, season with salt and pepper, and add enough cold water (6-8 tablespoonfuls) to make a smooth elastic dough. Transfer the dough to a lightly floured board and divide it into 12 small dumplings, pop them on to the soup – don't press them down, though, just let them float. Then put the lid back on and simmer for a further 25 minutes. Taste to check the seasoning and ladle the goulash into six warmed, deep bowls, making sure everyone has 2 dumplings. Finish each one with a spoonful of soured cream and a sprinkling of paprika.

The London Particular (yellow split pea soup)
Serves 6

3½ pints (2 litres) ham, bacon or vegetable stock

12 oz (350 g) yellow (or green) split peas (no need to soak)

3 oz (75 g) butter

6 oz (175 g) smoked streaky bacon, derinded and diced

1 medium onion, roughly chopped

1 celery stalk, chopped

1 large carrot, peeled and sliced

salt and freshly milled black pepper

To serve

crispy bacon bits (see recipe)

2 oz (50 g) crustless white bread, cut into ⅓ inch (8 mm) cubes for small croutons

This soup which can be made with ham or bacon stock from boiled smoked bacon, is so named because of the thick, dense 'peasouper' London fogs that were so prevalent during the first half of the last century.

First of all, pour the stock into your largest saucepan (about 8 pints/4.5 litres) and bring just up to simmering point, then add the split peas, stir well and simmer very gently for about 30 minutes. Meanwhile, heat 1 oz (25 g) of the butter in a medium saucepan and add 4 oz (110 g) of the bacon, along with the prepared vegetables. Cook them over a medium heat until softened and nicely golden – this will take about 15 minutes.

After that, the bacon and softened vegetables can be transferred to join the stock and split peas. Then add some salt and freshly milled pepper, put the lid on and simmer very gently for a further 40-50 minutes.

Meanwhile, heat a large frying pan (without any fat in it) and fry the remaining bacon until it is really crisp, then transfer it to a plate using a draining spoon. Next add 1 oz (25 g) of the butter to the pan, and as soon as it begins to foam, add the cubes of bread and fry these, tossing them around, for about five minutes until they are also nice and crisp.

When the soup is ready, leave it to cool a little, then process it in a food processor or blender in batches (you will find a large bowl is helpful here to put the soup in as it is ready). When it is all puréed, return it to the saucepan. Taste to check the seasoning, adding just a little more stock or water if it seems a little too thick. Just before serving, melt the remaining butter into it, then ladle into serving bowls and sprinkle each one with the croutons and crispy bacon bits.

Stocks and Garnishes

Fresh stocks are now available in tubs from supermarkets, but if you need a large quantity, these can be expensive. There are very good powdered vegetable stocks, such as Marigold Swiss Vegetable Bouillon Powder, which has only pure vegetable flavour. Miso is a useful storecupboard standby for an instant oriental stock (see pages 22 and 33). Here's how to make a few stocks – they can all be frozen.

Beef stock
Makes about 4 pints (2.25 litres)

For a light beef stock, use the same ingredients and follow the same instructions but leave out the initial roasting of the bones and vegetables.

3 lb (about 1.35 kg) beef bones, in pieces

2 large carrots, peeled and cut into chunks

2 onions, quartered

3 celery stalks, each cut into three pieces

a few parsley stalks

1 bay leaf

8 whole black peppercorns

1 blade of mace

1 sprig of fresh thyme

1 teaspoon salt

Pre-heat the oven to gas mark 8, 450°F (230°C).

Begin by placing the bones in a large roasting tin, tucking the peeled chunks of carrot, quartered onion and the pieces of celery in among them.

Now, without adding any fat, just pop the roasting tin on to a high shelf in the oven and leave it there for 45 minutes, basting with the juices now and then. After that, the bones and the vegetables will have turned brown at the edges.

Now transfer them all to the very largest saucepan you own, add enough cold water just to cover everything - about 4-5 pints (2.25-2.8 litres) - and add the rest of the ingredients, then as soon as it reaches boiling point, remove the scum and lower the heat. Put the lid on but not completely as it's best to leave a little gap for the steam to escape, which will help to reduce and concentrate the stock as it simmers away. Leave the stock to cook very gently on a low heat for about 4 hours.

When the stock is ready, you need to leave it to become quite cold. Then, using a slotted spoon, remove the fat that will have congealed on the surface. The stock is now ready to use. ➤

Chicken stock
Makes about 1½ pints (850 ml)

1 set of chicken giblets
or a couple of chicken wings and tips

1 stick of celery, cut in half
and split lengthways

2 small carrots, split lengthways

2 small onions, sliced

2 bay leaves

12 black peppercorns

1 small bunch of parsley stalks
and celery leaves

a pinch of salt

Place the giblets and the other ingredients in a saucepan with 2 pints (1.2 litres) cold water, cover and bring to the boil. Simmer briskly for 1 hour, then strain the stock.

Ham stock
Makes about 3½ pints (2 litres)

the bones and scraps of a ham

2 celery sticks (plus leaves)

1 large carrot and 1 leek, split lengthways

6 black peppercorns

a few parsley stalks

1 bay leaf

1 sprig of fresh thyme

Place all the ingredients in a saucepan and add 4 pints (2.25 litres) cold water. Bring everything up to simmering point, remove any scum from the surface and simmer gently, covered, for 1½-2 hours. Then strain the stock.

Fish stock
Makes about 1 pint (570 ml)

1 lb (450 g) fish trimmings

5 fl oz (150 ml) dry white wine

1 onion, quartered

2 celery stalks, chopped

a few sprigs of fresh parsley and 1 of fresh thyme

1 bay leaf

salt and freshly milled black pepper

Place the trimmings in a large pan, with 1 pint (570 ml) water and the rest of the ingredients, season, then simmer for about 20 minutes, without a lid, and strain.

Shellfish stock

Make as above, substituting whatever shells you have left after peeling prawns, for the 1 lb (450 g) fish trimmings.

Vegetable stock
Makes about 1 pint (570 ml)

1 stick of celery, cut in half and split lengthways

2 small carrots, split in half lengthways

2 small onions, sliced

2 bay leaves

12 black peppercorns

1 small bunch of parsley stalks and celery leaves

a pinch of salt

Place all the ingredients in a saucepan with 1-1½ pints (570-850 ml) cold water, cover, and boil briskly for 30 minutes. Then strain, discarding the vegetables.

Croutons
Serves 4

Crisp, golden croutons are lovely sprinkled over the top of a bowl of hot or chilled soup. You can make croutons a day ahead, and store them in an airtight container once they have cooled.

2 oz (50 g) bread, cut into small cubes

1 tablespoon olive oil

Pre-heat the oven to gas mark 4, 350°F (180°C).

Just place the cubes of bread in a bowl, together with the oil, and stir them around so that they get an even coating. Then arrange them on a baking sheet. Bake them on a high shelf in the oven for 10 minutes or until they are crisp and golden. One word of warning: do use a kitchen timer for this operation because it's actually very hard to bake something for just 10 minutes without forgetting all about it. Then cool on the baking sheet and store in an airtight container.

Garlic croutons
Serves 4

Follow the recipe for plain croutons (above), only this time add 1 crushed clove of garlic to the bowl, along with the olive oil and cubes of bread. Stir them around and bake on a baking sheet, as above, for 10 minutes (remember to put a timer on). Leave to cool and store in an airtight container until you are ready to use them.

Parmesan croutons
Serves 4

Follow the recipe for plain croutons (left), placing the oil and cubes of bread in a small bowl and stirring them around until the oil is soaked up, then sprinkle in 1 dessertspoon of freshly grated Parmesan. Stir the cubes around to coat them in that as well, then spread them on the baking sheet and bake on a high shelf for 10 minutes (remembering to put a timer on). Cool and store the croutons in an airtight container.

Olive ciabatta croutons
Serves 4

4 medium slices ciabatta bread (about 2 oz/50 g) each

1 tablespoon olive oil

1 dessertspoon olive paste

Pre-heat the oven to gas mark 5, 375°F (190°C).

First of all, cut the slices of ciabatta bread into small cubes. Then place the cubes of bread in a bowl, together with the olive oil and the dessertspoon of olive paste. Stir the cubes around to get a good coating of the olive oil paste.

Next, arrange the croutons on a small baking sheet and put them in the oven to bake for 8-10 minutes - remember to set the kitchen timer. Then leave the croutons to cool on the baking sheet and store them in an airtight container until you are ready to use them. ➤

Other ideas

Here are a few other quick and easy
suggestions that you might like to try
when serving soups.

Add a spoonful of freshly snipped
chives or other herbs, or some finely
chopped chilli or spring onions
(including the green bits), to the bottom
of each bowl before ladling in soup,
or sprinkle on to each bowl as a garnish
before serving.

A marbling of cream, crème fraîche,
yoghurt or fromage frais (particularly if
you are watching the calories) can be
swirled in just before you're ready to
serve hot or chilled soup.

Plenty of freshly grated Parmesan
cheese or slices of crusty French bread,
topped with a melting cheese, such
as Fontina or Gruyère, then browned
under the grill, are lovely additions to
warming winter soups.

Sprouts, shallots and leeks are
delicious finely shredded and then lightly
fried in a little oil in a very hot pan before
sprinkling over soups

Smoked bacon or pancetta, cut into
cubes or sliced thinly, then fried till crisp
and golden, makes another excellent
garnish.

Salsas or paper-thin slices of
cucumber or fruit, such as apple or
halved grapes, are a nice idea, especially
when you're making low-fat soups.

Vegetable Crisps

If you're entertaining, crisps made
with root vegetables, such as parsnips
or sweet potato, are rather special.

1 medium to large parsnip or sweet potato
(10-12 oz/275-350 g)
6 tablespoons groundnut or other flavourless oil
salt

First, peel the parsnip or sweet potato and
then slice it into rounds as thinly as you
possibly can, using a sharp knife or a
mandoline, which is ideal for this job.
Now heat the oil in a large frying pan
until it is very hot, almost smoking, then
fry the slices in batches until they are
golden brown, about 2-3 minutes. They
will not stay flat or colour evenly but will
twist into lovely shapes (see right).

As they're cooked, remove them with
a slotted spoon and spread them out on
kitchen paper to drain. Sprinkle lightly
with salt. If you like, you can make these
in advance, as they will stay crisp for a
couple of hours.

Equipment

You don't need a lot of special equipment
for making soups at home except for a
food processor, blender or alternatively, a
hand-held blender. A blender is excellent
for puréeing smooth, elegant soups
whereas a food processor is fine when you
want to have a bit of texture in the soup.

Conversions for Australia and New Zealand

Measurements in this book refer to British standard imperial and metric measurements.

The standard UK teaspoon measure is 5 ml, the dessertspoon is 10 ml and the tablespoon measure is 15 ml. In Australia, the standard tablespoon is 20 ml.

UK large eggs weigh 63-73 g.

Converting standard cups to imperial and metric weights

Ingredients (1 cup)	Imperial/metric
black beans, dried	8 oz /225 g
butter	9 oz/250 g
cabbage, shredded	3 oz/75 g
cannellini beans, dried	7 oz/200 g
carrots, finely chopped	5 oz/150 g
caster sugar	9 oz/250 g
celery, sliced	4½ oz/125 g
Cheddar, grated*	4½ oz/125 g
chickpeas, dried	8 oz/225 g
coriander, chopped	2 oz/50 g
couscous	6½ oz/185 g
demerara sugar	8 oz/225 g
flour, plain or self raising	4½ oz/125 g
flour, wholemeal	5 oz/150 g
granulated sugar	9 oz/250 g
haricot beans, dried	7 oz/200 g
leeks, sliced	4 oz /110 g
lentils, brown-green	6½ oz/185 g
mushrooms, sliced	3½ oz/95 g
nuts, chopped	5 oz/150 g
onion, chopped	5 oz/150 g
parsley, flat leaf, whole	¾ oz/20 g
Parmesan, finely grated	4 oz/110 g
peas, fresh, shelled	5 oz /150 g
pumpkin, ½ inch/1 cm dice	5 oz /150 g
rice, raw, short grain	7½ oz/210 g
rice, raw, long grain	7 oz/200 g
soft brown sugar	8 oz/225 g
spinach, raw, baby English*	2 oz/50 g
split peas, dried	8 oz/225 g
tomatoes, fresh, chopped	7 oz/200 g
tomatoes, tinned, chopped	9 oz/250 g

* Firmly packed

Liquid cup conversions

Imperial	Metric	Cups
1 fl oz	25 ml	⅛ cup
2 fl oz	55 ml	¼ cup
2¾ fl oz	80 ml	⅓ cup
4 fl oz	125 ml	½ cup
6 fl oz	185 ml	¾ cup
8 fl oz	250 ml	1 cup
10 fl oz	275 ml	1¼ cups
12 fl oz	375 ml	1½ cups
16 fl oz	500 ml	2 cups
1 pint	570 ml	2½ cups
24 fl oz	750 ml	3 cups
32 fl oz	1 litre	4 cups

A few ingredient names

aubergine
eggplant

Bramley apple
green cooking apple

courgettes
zucchini

fine green beans
French green beans

marrow
large zucchini

open-cap mushrooms
flat-cap mushrooms

pepper, red/yellow/green
capsicum

shallots
eschalot/French shallot

spinach
English spinach

tomato purée
tomato paste

Index

Steve Baxter 83
Jean Cazals 34, 110
Patrice de Villiers 102
Miki Duisterhof 5, 6, 14/15, 23, 28,
34, 38, 60, 64, 68, 76, 89, 93, 94, 118,
121, 131, 133
Norman Hollands 71
Peter Knab 6, 10, 13, 16, 19, 20, 23,
30/31, 34, 42, 48, 52, 56, 59, 67, 71,
89, 94, 98, 101, 105, 117, 126
Jonathan Lovekin 27, 34, 52, 113
Jason Lowe 101
J P Masclet 137
S & O Matthews 6, 28, 34, 60, 79, 94
Gareth Morgans 23, 28, 83, 89, 131
David Munns 76, 117, 126
Debbie Patterson 84/85
Michael Paul 24, 41, 72
Dan Stevens 60, 90
Kevin Summers 60, 94
Simon Walton 9, 10, 32, 38, 45,
52, 55, 59, 63, 80, 86, 101, 106, 110,
122, 131
Cameron Watt 6, 16, 28, 37, 38,
46/47, 51, 52, 59, 71, 74/75, 83, 89,
94, 97, 108/9, 110, 114, 117, 125
Rob White 10, 64, 76, 117
Tim Winter 6, 34, 94

Delia Smith is Britain's best-selling cookery author, whose books have sold over 16 million copies. Delia's other books include *How To Cook Books One*, *Two* and *Three*, her *Vegetarian Collection*, the *Complete Illustrated Cookery Course*, *One Is Fun*, the *Summer* and *Winter Collections* and *Christmas*. She has launched her own website. She is also a director of Norwich City Football Club, where she is in charge of Canary Catering, several restaurants and a regular series of food and wine workshops.

She is married to the writer and editor Michael Wynn Jones and they live in Suffolk.

For more information on Delia's restaurant,
food and wine workshops and events, contact:
Delia's Canary Catering, Norwich City Football Club, Carrow Road,
Norwich NR1 1JE; www.deliascanarycatering.co.uk
For Delia's Canary Catering (conferencing and events enquiries),
telephone 01603 218704
For Delia's Restaurant and Bar (reservations),
telephone 01603 218705

Visit Delia's website at www.deliaonline.com